The Foster Carer's Handbook on Education

GETTING THE BEST FOR YOUR CHILD

Sarah Alix

With Eileen Fursland and Nicola Hill

Published by
CoramBAAF Adoption and Fostering Academy
41 Brunswick Square
London WC1N 1AZ
www.corambaaf.org.uk

Coram Academy Limited, registered as a company limited by guarantee in England and Wales number 9697712, part of the Coram group, charity number 312278

British Library Cataloguing in Publication Data
A catalogue record for this book is available from the British Library

ISBN 978 1 910039 87 8

Project management by Miranda Davies, CoramBAAF
Designed by Helen Joubert Design
Printed in Great Britain by The Lavenham Press

Trade distribution by Turnaround Publisher Services, Unit 3, Olympia Trading Estate, Coburg Road, London N22 6TZ

Contents

Acknowledgements

I would like to thank Shaila Shah and CoramBAAF for commissioning this book. In particular, my extended thanks go to Miranda Davies for her hard work and dedication in guiding and editing this book through all its many stages.

A big thank you is also due to Alan Fisher for his work on this project. His input has been invaluable and I am very grateful for the work he completed, especially his contribution to Chapter 2.

I am eternally grateful to Eileen Fursland and Nicola Hill for their support and the writing of elements of this book. Eileen's companion handbook for adopters provided much of the text in Chapters 1 and 5–8 while Nicola commented on the whole book as well as writing Chapter 10 and the section on LGBTQ+ young people in Chapter 8. Between them they have brought a wealth of experience in a range of contexts.

Further thanks to Katie Jones, foster carer, and Fiona Darlington Black, Head of Services for Cornerways Fostering in Surrey, for their expert comments on the script.

I would finally like to thank all of the children in care and their foster carers with whom I have worked throughout my career in education. The insight into their lives, the challenges they face and the decisions they need to make surrounding their education have given me the passion to strive for a better understanding of the support needed in this area and its impact on their future lives.

About the authors

Sarah Alix has worked for 20 years in education as a youth worker, class teacher, local authority behaviour support adviser and as a Senior Lecturer and Deputy Head of Department with Anglia Ruskin University. She is currently the Academic Programme Director for North Essex Teacher Training (NETT) and a Senior Fellow of the Higher Education Academy.

Sarah completed her Doctorate of Education at Brunel University. Her thesis examined the perceptions and experiences of trainee teachers and their mentors working with looked after children, focusing on the concept of training for teachers working with children in care.

Her previous publications (all for the Chartered College of Teaching) include: *How Trainee Teachers are Trained to Support Looked After Children: A model of development* (online, 2018); *The Impact of Introducing Thinking Skills through Philosophy 4 Children* (2018); and *How Do Pupil Responses to Peer Assessment and Feedback Impact on their Literacy Progression*? (co-authored with Florence Pullon, 2019).

Eileen Fursland is a freelance writer specialising in issues affecting children and young people. She has written extensively for BAAF (now CoramBAAF) on a number of publications since 2002, as well as for a range of magazines and national newspapers and other organisations.

Eileen's publications for BAAF include the training course *Preparing to Adopt* (she wrote the first edition in 2002 with a working party from BAAF which devised the course, and the fourth edition, 2014, with Nicky Probert and Elaine Dibben); *Facing up to Facebook* (second edition, 2013); *Social Networking and Contact* (2010); *Foster Care and Social Networking* (2011); *Social Networking and You* (2011); and *Ten Top Tips on Supporting Education*, with Kate Cairns and Chris Stanway. In earlier collaborations with Kate Cairns, she co-wrote BAAF's training programmes: *Trauma and Recovery*; *Safer Caring*; *Building Identity*; and *Transitions and Endings*. Most recently she wrote three books in this series: *The Adopter's Handbook on Therapy* (2016), *Caring for a Child who has been Sexually Exploited* (2018) and *The Adopter's Handbook on Education* (2018) that acts as a companion guide to this book.

Nicola Hill has been a freelance writer and editor for over 20 years. As well as numerous articles in the *Guardian*, she is the author of three books: *A Very Pink Wedding* (Collins, 2007), *The Pink Guide to Adoption* (third edition, CoramBAAF, 2020) and *Proud Parents* (BAAF, 2013). Since 2010, she has been a foster carer for two children; at the time of writing, one is at university and the other studying for A-levels. Nicola is a member of Hackney Council's Virtual School management committee and Tower Hamlets' adoption and fostering panels. She has a BSc in Social Psychology from the London School of Economics.

Introduction

> *School had never been important to me, but my foster carer had this thing about education, and she really pushed me. She expected a lot from me and she made me want to achieve things – both for me and for her. And she'd go and speak to the school if she felt they weren't supporting me like they ought to. She was a total tiger, fighting for me like her cub!*
>
> (Elinor, quoted in Bond, 2016, p. 75)

As a foster carer you have a central role to play in the education of the children and young people you look after. Whatever their age, ability or situation, your commitment can make a huge difference to their attitudes to learning, their achievements and state of mind, and how they get on in later life.

The following figures show why your interest and support are so important:

- Sixty-three per cent of looked after children achieved level 2 or above compared to 88 per cent of non-looked after children.
- Fifty-two per cent of looked after children achieved level 4 or above in reading, writing and mathematics, compared to 80 per cent of all children.
- Fourteen per cent of looked after children achieved 5+ A*–Cs (including English and maths) at GCSE, compared to 53 per cent of all children.
- Only six per cent go to university compared with nearly 50 per cent of children nationally.
- Looked after children are five times as likely to be excluded from school.
- Half of looked after children have emotional, behavioural and health problems.

(Children's Commissioner, 2017; Department for Education, 2015; 2016)

But all is not lost. Despite this grim picture, outcomes across all ages are getting better and with increased understanding and support from foster carers, teachers and others, a lot more can be done to improve the situation.

Of course there are many types of fostering: emergency, short-break, remand and fostering for adoption as well as kinship care, short- and long-term foster care. This book applies mainly to the last three arrangements where children aged five or above are likely to be attending a particular school for some time.

When a child is placed in *short-term care,* even if he[1] remains at his present school, the changes in his home life are bound to be unsettling and can affect his ability to focus on schoolwork. It is therefore important for carers to keep communicating with teachers and support the child with homework. If a child moves to a new school, this has a greater impact and it will take time for him to settle in and make friends. Changes of school, however brief, can directly affect educational progress.

Children in *long-term care* may well experience similar challenges. Settling in and making new friends are just two of the issues they face. Records need to be swiftly passed between schools so that teachers have an understanding of their strengths and weaknesses, whether they need extra support and in which areas, and what part of the curriculum they have covered so far.

This handbook aims to help you support the education of the children and young people you foster, however short or long term this may be. Much of the information and advice is likely to apply to children's experiences of school across the four countries of the UK. However, their educational systems vary. Scotland has its own regulatory structure, its own set of exams and curriculum, and a wider, more flexible approach. England, Wales and Northern Ireland are broadly similar with occasional variations. This book refers to the framework in England (Fursland, 2018).[2]

The neglect, abuse and loss that cause so many looked after children to be separated from their birth parents can shape the way in which they see themselves, other people and the world around them. This, in turn, can have a major effect on their experiences of school, both in terms of the demands of the curriculum and the social and emotional pressures of school life. Before going into detail about what you, as a foster carer, can do, it is important to

1 Children are referred to as "he" or "she" in every other chapter throughout the book.

2 For more information about education in the devolved countries visit: www.learning.wales.gov.uk(Wales); https://education.gov.scot (Scotland); and www.deni.gov.uk (Northern Ireland).

understand how your child's early experiences might affect his ability to cope with school life and readiness to learn.

Most of you will be familiar with the concepts of developmental trauma, attachment difficulties and Foetal Alcohol Spectrum Disorders (FASD). You will almost certainly have learned about and read about these in your training, but it may be helpful to understand how such a history can specifically affect children's experiences of the school system. We therefore open with a chapter adapted from CoramBAAF's companion guide, *The Adopter's Handbook on Education* (Fursland, 2018), which provides a brief explanation of the impact that early traumatic and difficult attachment experiences can have on a child's ability to cope with school life and learning.

Fostering comes with a number of obligations, including a commitment to supporting the education of the children in your care. Chapter 2 outlines the legal framework connecting care and education, in particular Standard 8 of the National Minimum Standards (NMS), which is dedicated to ensuring that 'children are supported to achieve their educational potential'.

The next chapters cover the all-important processes of planning, including Personal Education Plans (PEPS) and the roles and responsibilities of the team around the child. They explain how the school system works and the support available so that you can work with teachers, schools, social workers and even birth parents to make sure that the children and young people you are fostering achieve the best possible results, both in terms of qualifications and social and behavioural skills. The value of reading is emphasised, not only for language and literacy but across all other areas of learning and development, including the positive impact it can have on children's behaviour.

Helpful tips, strategies and questions are illustrated, where possible, by case studies, and key points summarise the content of each chapter. Useful contacts, including relevant websites, are listed at the end. You'll also find an appendix giving more details on different types of schools and a glossary to remind you of the meaning of certain common terms and abbreviations.

As Eileen Fursland has highlighted in her recent handbook for adopters, budget cuts and mounting pressure on teachers mean that many schools struggle to provide the extra support needed by some looked after children. But at the same time, there are positive developments like greater awareness of children's mental health needs and the effects of trauma and attachment difficulties. There is also more government support for designated teachers and "virtual schools", i.e. the overseeing bodies (not buildings) set up by local authorities to promote the progress and educational attainment of children and young people who are or have been in care (see Chapter 4).

Engaging with your foster child's school by communicating with teachers and encouraging their learning at home can hugely influence their future success. You don't need to know everything or be an expert, but if you understand how the school system works and know who to go to for information, advice and guidance, this will not only benefit your child but also, hopefully, make the task of fostering a little easier.

1 How early experiences can affect children's learning

At its best, school can be a place where children learn to become all that they can be; it can open the doors to discovery, inspiration and friendship, as well as providing a well-rounded education that equips each child with the knowledge and skills they need for life. But sadly that is not how it is for many fostered children whose early experiences have blocked their ability to learn and to manage school life.

Children who have experienced neglect and abuse – and those who have been damaged even before birth – have different needs from others their age. They need understanding and extra support in order to cope with just being at school as well as learning how to process ideas and information effectively. But carers and teachers often don't know how to work with them because these children's needs can go beyond what their training and experience, as teachers and foster carers, have prepared them for.

A child's experience of school can be a source of stress not only for the child herself but for her carers. Sometimes children manage to hold things together in school but explode when they get home and feel safe enough to release their frustration and anxiety. Carers often face the fall-out.

The impact of early experiences

The lives of fostered children, even when they are looked after in a loving and caring foster family, continue to be deeply affected by what happened to them early on. The neglect, abuse, chaotic environments and traumatic events that caused them to be removed from their birth families, and the grief and loss of disrupted attachments can shape how they see themselves, other people and the world around them. Children who have had a difficult start can be left with vulnerabilities and gaps in terms of their psychological and social development, and their ability to control their emotions and behaviours.

A child may be highly intelligent but unable to do well at school – or sometimes even cope with school at all – because of emotional, social and behavioural difficulties stemming from her early experiences. It is worrying and upsetting for carers to see that their child is stressed or unhappy in school, falling behind and struggling to make friends because of the trouble she has forming relationships, or because her unpredictable behaviour makes other children wary of her.

For some children and young people in foster care, harm was done before they were even born, when exposed to alcohol and/or drugs in the womb. Pre-natal exposure to alcohol, when a woman drinks during pregnancy, can damage the developing brain of the foetus. It can cause permanent problems, affecting the child's ability to concentrate, learn, remember and understand (Mather, 2018).

The impact of trauma and attachment difficulties

Every looked after child or young person has her own unique history but most have one thing in common: their early life experiences have been lacking in some way. Many have spent their first few months or years with parents who were unable to meet their needs. They may have been deprived of stimulation and affection, gone cold and hungry, or been emotionally, physically or sexually abused. They may be unused to boundaries and feel unsafe. Education may not have been fully supported or their attendance may have been erratic. Other children may have experienced patterns of care and attachment more attuned to their needs; certainly they may have been loved, but for whatever reason their families could not keep them safe and meet all their needs.

Repeated losses – being removed from the birth family home, being moved to different foster carers – can leave such children with unresolved grief and the constant fear that they will once again be taken away from everything they know. All fostered children will have experienced at least one disrupted or broken attachment. As a result, many develop an insecure attachment style: they relate to others in an anxious, avoidant, angry/ambivalent or disorganised way. They find it difficult to put their trust in adults, seek comfort, accept guidance, feel safe, make friends, empathise with others or achieve many of the everyday things that come easily to other children.

Children cannot learn if they feel unsafe, if they cannot trust their teacher or if they are too afraid of rejection and failure to try and learn new things.

Building a new attachment with a child or young person you are looking after can take a long time. And at school, your child has to spend long periods of time away from you and share the teacher's attention with many other pupils. This can trigger her attachment needs or attachment-related trauma, as she wonders whether you will still be there when she gets home and whether you will have forgotten her.

Teachers are becoming much more aware of the importance of attachment, and children who used to be seen as "clingy, attention-seeking and disruptive" are now being recognised as "attachment-seeking".

Here are two short case studies showing how attachment difficulties can play out in the classroom:

> *Ten-year-old Amber... would regularly shout out in class and often follow the teacher round the room. Through a thorough assessment, it emerged that Amber had previously been starved of adult attention and had been significantly neglected. She had learned various survival strategies for being kept in the minds of others; her shouting out was her way of communicating, 'Don't forget me, please remember me.'*
>
> *Five-year-old Dylan had experienced unavailable/absent parenting. He had learned to conceal, internalise and/or deny his emotions. Within the classroom this showed itself as Dylan being overly self-reliant and compliant. He avoided teacher support, seemingly from fear of being rejected or ignored. This, in turn, made him fall under the radar and appear "invisible", and once again mirrored his early experiences of being forgotten and neglected. This reinforced Dylan's insecure avoidant-attachment style and his expectations of being ignored, invisible and unimportant.*
>
> (Treisman, 2017, p. 148)

School requires children and young people to trust adults and give up control to them – something that those who have experienced abuse at the hands of trusted adults can find particularly difficult. This can go against the defence and "survival strategies" they may have developed in their birth families.

Children and young people's difficulties also affect their relationships with other children. Sometimes their emotional and behavioural needs can make it hard for them to make and keep friends. If a child or young person is withdrawn or too controlling, often lashes out or has meltdowns, or has not learned to take turns and share, other children will tend to avoid her.

Feeling unsafe

The feeling of lack of safety described earlier can result in children becoming "hypervigilant" or "dissociating" at times of stress. When they feel unsafe (which may be much of the time while they are at school), children can be on high alert, constantly in "fight" mode and preoccupied with possible threats. This means that they may overreact to things such as someone touching them or appearing suddenly behind them, which can lead them to "kick off" in the classroom; if the teacher doesn't understand, the child is likely to find herself in trouble.

In other children, or at other times, the child "zones out", withdraws and becomes dissociated from everything going on around her. The teacher may interpret this as simply not paying attention, daydreaming, and so on.

Such children may even do certain things without consciously realising what they are doing, which again can get them into trouble.

Dysregulation

If babies have not been cared for by an adult who is attuned to their emotions, who is there to soothe them and comfort them when they are upset, they will not develop the ability to reliably regulate their own emotions. They can quickly become overwhelmed by feelings of stress and fear (which may play out as anger).

Dysregulated behaviour can look different for every child. In the classroom it might mean fidgeting, making repetitive noises, calling out, chattering and giggling, lashing out, becoming withdrawn and even things like urinating somewhere inappropriate. A dysregulated child is liable to flare up, over-react to seemingly small things, or become overwhelmed in stressful situations. These behaviours, of course, often don't go down well in the classroom or with peers.

Chronological age vs developmental age

Gaps in children's development can mean that they feel, think and act much younger than they really are. In school, children and young people often suffer because people's expectations are based on their years rather than their developmental age – and some are still operating at the emotional age of a toddler or much younger child.

These children need teachers who understand this and can provide the right learning and play activities, supervision, boundaries and targets.

Executive functioning difficulties

Many children and young people have problems with "executive functioning". This refers to the ability to organise, concentrate, set goals, plan tasks, process information, solve problems, switch focus from one task to another, and remember information and instructions. It is easy to see how such problems make school life and learning challenging for them. They may forget to bring into school the things they need, they have trouble concentrating or switching from one task to another, and find it hard to finish work in the time allowed.

Sensory issues and triggers

Developmental trauma affects the ability to take in and process the information received from the senses – sights, sound, smell, touch, taste, body awareness and balance. As babies and toddlers, children may have been ignored or grossly under-stimulated or left alone feeling cold, wet and hungry, and may not have had the opportunity to play with toys or explore their surroundings.

Some children with FASD also have sensory processing difficulties (see below). This means they may be unable to recognise when they are too cold, too warm, hungry or thirsty. Some are over-sensitive to sensory input and can't cope with busy, bright and noisy classrooms. Certain smells and tastes can seem overpowering to them. Even their clothes may feel scratchy and uncomfortable.

When a child or young person has sensory issues, the clamour of the classroom, the crowds in the corridor, the shouting in the playground and the queue in the dining hall can leave her feeling too stressed to function or even, sometimes, unwilling to go to school at all.

Trauma triggers and curriculum issues

In many children who have been abused and traumatised, certain things can trigger traumatic memories. For example, this may be sounds, smells, people who look something like their abuser, places (e.g. school showers, being in the woods) or the time of year (e.g. autumn leaves or snow) or the sight of a police officer that may remind them of when they were removed from the birth family home.

Examples of areas that can be tricky include: being asked to bring in pictures of the child as a baby (which you may not have); writing about her early life; assemblies about maltreated children (e.g. by the NSPCC); and being asked to do a family tree.

Lessons about drugs and alcohol can stir up unhappy memories of birth relatives and also make a child or young person worry about developing the same problems. Sex education lessons could be uncomfortable or upsetting for a child who was sexually abused in early life, as could lessons about the effect of alcohol in pregnancy, especially for young people with FASD.

Understanding the effects of FASD

FASD is a complex disability that is only recently becoming better understood in the UK. Children and indeed adults with FASD have a range of difficulties and require some degree of support for life. Each individual with FASD may have some or all of a variety of mental and physical challenges – to a degree or on a "spectrum" from mild to very severe.

The difficulties may not become apparent until the child starts school, or even later. Sometimes children do reasonably well in primary school but the complex demands of secondary education leave them unable to cope. They find any kind of change disruptive and destabilising.

Diagnostic services are patchy. Even with a diagnosis and an awareness of the condition, supporting children with FASD in school can be a challenge for the child's teachers.

Brian Roberts is head teacher of a virtual school and a trainer; he and his wife are foster carers who took out special guardianship orders for a sibling group of three girls, all affected by FASD. He says the impact on a child's ability to learn is poorly understood, even by many people closely linked to their education. These children struggle to conform to the rules and social norms of school. Traditional learning strategies need to be amended to allow affected children to reach their full potential.

Roberts gives the following three examples of the challenges:

- *At the beginning of Year 11, a 15-year-old boy took a knife into his secondary school. He had picked up the knife when carpets were being fitted in his home and liked it so much that he wanted to show his friends. It was so important to him that he showed it to the first person he met at the school gate. Unfortunately, it was a Police Community Support Officer. The boy was permanently excluded, could not cope in the Pupil Referral Unit and at the end of Year 11 ended up with no qualifications. Most teachers would argue that this is not the typical behaviour of an adolescent who decided to take a knife into school. "Innocent delinquency" is the term often used to describe this type of behaviour, which is characteristic of the FASD child.*
- *An 11-year-old girl upset her maths teacher by "rudely" answering back in class in response to being told off for her behaviour and attitude. When the teacher attempted to quieten her by asking whether she thought the "silly" comment she had made was funny, the "rude" answer was 'Yes, that's why I did it.' The child's reasoning was that the teacher had asked her a question and it would be rude not to answer and even ruder to lie...The FASD child frequently fails to understand adult sarcasm and often misinterprets everyday social communication.*
- *In nursery school, a three-year-old would scream and run away from the teaching assistant every time he saw her. This was after experiencing a whole day at nursery based on The Gruffalo children's story when the teaching assistant had dressed up as the Gruffalo. As a few of the younger children had been frightened, in order to reassure them the teaching assistant removed the costume's head. Most of the children were reassured except for this boy who was convinced that the teaching assistant was the Gruffalo. Distinguishing fantasy from reality can be a continuing struggle for the FASD child.*

  (Roberts, 2015, p. 237)

It's important, as with all children, to see their strengths as well as their difficulties:

- *Students with FASD are often ambitious and have a range of practical strengths which are useful in their educational careers and throughout life.*
- *Many are articulate and have engaging personalities. They enjoy being with other people.*

- *Many have learning strengths around literacy and practical subjects, such as art, performing arts, sport, and technologies, although they often have difficulties with comprehension.*
- *While they have working/short-term memory difficulties, rote learning and long-term memory can be strengths.*

(NOFAS-UK, 2017)

NOFAS-UK (National Organisation for Foetal Alcohol Syndrome UK) has an excellent downloadable guide to help teachers to support learners affected by FASD in school, called *Teaching a Student with FASD* (see www.nofas-uk.org).

Difficulty in diagnosis

It may not be possible, or at least not early on, to get a firm diagnosis to explain the cause of a child's particular difficulties. The symptoms of many conditions can look a lot like each other. Finding the root of the problem is not always straightforward.

Obtaining a diagnosis of a particular condition may need assessment by a specialist – for example, a paediatrician for attention deficit hyperactivity disorder (ADHD), an occupational therapist or sensory integration expert for sensory integration disorders, a speech and language therapist for communication problems, and an educational psychologist for other issues such as executive functioning problems and specific learning difficulties such as dyslexia and dyspraxia. Getting your child's needs recognised, diagnosed and agreed by the various professionals and panels can be a long and trying process.

Traumatic stress in childhood seems to be linked to conditions like depression, anxiety, ADHD and conduct (behaviour) disorders. Children can also be subject to a range of other difficulties such as developmental delay, speech and language issues and specific learning difficulties.

Responding to needs, whatever the underlying cause

The child's experience in her mother's womb (if the mother drank alcohol and/or took drugs in pregnancy), genetic influences, early attachment experiences and neglect or abuse in childhood can contribute to the way she functions.

For example, children with attachment difficulties as well as those with FASD may be anxious about change and find it unsettling, become stressed and overwhelmed by aspects of school life and find it less easy than their peers to form friendships with other children.

If you can get one, a diagnosis can be helpful because it may well make it easier for everyone around the child to understand why she has these particular problems or behaves as she does. Hopefully, it should also encourage teachers to have different expectations of the child and to take the appropriate approach. But unfortunately it won't necessarily lead to support or therapy. The school should already be providing for any learning needs the child has, no matter what the cause.

In more severe cases of special educational needs and disability, a child who meets the threshold will have an Education, Health and Care (EHC) plan that outlines the extra support she should receive, or in some cases, the special school she needs to go to (see Chapter 9).

Key points

- Children's early experiences can have a very big impact on their development, including their ability and readiness to learn. Teachers are beginning to understand this, especially the role that attachment plays in how children cope with expressing and controlling their emotions, but there is still a long way to go.
- Children with early experiences of neglect or other abuse may feel, think and act much younger than their age. It is important that the school's expectations don't exceed your child's stage of development.
- The child in your care may have problems with "executive functioning", i.e. the ability to organise. Again, this needs to be recognised and understood.
- A significant number of looked after children are likely to have some degree of FASD resulting from their mothers having drunk alcohol/taken drugs in pregnancy. Diagnosis isn't easy but there are a growing number of resources to help you identify whether this might apply to your child and, if so, what it can mean (see list at the end of this book).

2 Connecting care and education: the legal framework

The previous chapter briefly explained how troubled backgrounds and difficult early attachment experiences can affect looked after children and young people's ability to cope with school life and learning. This understanding is gradually gaining ground in schools and has resulted in increased government recognition of the importance of supporting the education of looked after children. Welcome initiatives include the Pupil Premium Plus and statutory guidance extending the role of designated teachers (Department for Education, 2018).

For carers and their fostering service, the key documents you need to know about are the Fostering Regulations and the National Minimum Standards for Fostering (NMS). These concern all fostering services, whether provided by local authorities or independent fostering providers (sometimes called fostering agencies). They therefore apply to all foster carers.

The Regulations are part of the Care Standards Act 2000. This means that they have the force of law and *must* be complied with. The NMS establish in detail the *minimum* expectations required of staff and carers in the fostering service.

In this chapter we look at Fostering Regulations in general before going on to consider individual Standards and what they mean for you as a foster carer. We then go on to pick out those which are particularly relevant to education.

Each one is connected to a desired outcome. For instance, Standard 8, cited in the Introduction, covers education in detail on the basis that:

> *The education and achievement of children is actively promoted as valuable in itself and as part of their preparation for adulthood. Children are supported to achieve their educational potential.*

The NMS require *active* promotion of education. Carers and other professionals must not sit back. Rather, it is up to them to show what support they are offering and how this encourages the child or young person to reach his full potential.

Looked after children and young people deserve all possible support and encouragement towards fulfilling their aspirations. Achievement is defined as realising their potential, rather than being measured in terms of exam results or certificates. Education is about the child as an individual and about recognising that potential, whatever his ability.

The safety, protection and well-being of looked after children are governed by a statutory and procedural framework that applies to everyone with a connection to the child or young person. This includes social workers, other professionals, the birth family and, of course, foster carers.

It may seem like a big leap from the law of the land to the day-to-day activities in a foster home but it is worth taking a moment or two to bridge that gap. The NMS in particular define in great depth what is expected of foster carers – day in, day out. They form the basis of your policy and procedure manuals. It is essential that you know what is expected of you: what you *must* do and what constitutes good foster care practice. If, of course, you are already familiar with the Standards outlined here, please go straight to Chapter 3 on planning and the team around the child.

Carers are not alone. These same Regulations and Standards give the fostering service a duty to support, guide and advise you. Supervising social workers (SSWs) are there to help explain the requirements and guidance in practice.

Also, the Regulations and NMS form the basis of Ofsted inspections. The service *must* comply with the Regulations, and they follow the Standards as if there were the same element of compulsion. That said, Minimum Standards do not mean standard provision across the board. They are designed to apply to the wide variety of fostering services and aim to enable each service to develop its own ethos and approach to meeting children's needs. Each service sets out its principles and the ways it will achieve its aims in its Statement of Purpose.

Your fostering service will have put in place a series of quality assurance measures to show not just that carers and staff are doing what they are supposed to be doing, but also that they can prove it; that is, show evidence that they are providing high quality foster care. This requirement is the origin of the many forms and formats, such as logs and Strengths and Difficulties Questionnaires, which carers and staff have to complete.

The NMS were extensively revised in 2011 after consultation with stakeholders, including children and young people and foster carers. They therefore incorporate suggestions and insights from carers.

From principles to practice

All legislation that applies to looked after children is imbued with three principles that stem from the Children Act 1989.

These are:

1. The child's welfare is paramount.
2. The child's wishes and feelings must be taken into consideration.
3. The child's culture, origin, background and religion must be taken into consideration.

These threads run through every decision, each procedure and all fostering practice. They form the foundation of child care practice in this country.

The best guide to the foundation of fostering practice is the statement of values that opens the NMS, or as they put it, 'the important principles which underpin these standards'. They are often missed in the hurry to get to the "doing" parts of the Standards, but pausing for a moment is worthwhile because they shape best practice and answer questions about what carers should do, why and how. These apply to fostering in general, not just education:

- *The child's welfare, safety and needs are at the centre of their care.*
- *Children should have an enjoyable childhood, benefiting from excellent parenting and education, enjoying a wide range of opportunities to develop their talents and skills leading to a successful adult life.*
- *Children are entitled to grow up in a loving environment that can meet their developmental needs.*
- *Every child should have his or her wishes and feelings listened to and taken into account.*

- *Each child should be valued as an individual and given personalised support in line with their individual needs and background in order to develop their identity, self-confidence and self-worth.*
- *The particular needs of disabled children and children with complex needs will be fully recognised and taken into account.*
- *The significance of contact for looked after children, and of maintaining relationships with birth parents and the wider family, including siblings, half-siblings and grandparents, is recognised, as is the foster carer's role in this.*
- *Children in foster care deserve to be treated as a good parent would treat their own children and to have the opportunity for as full an experience of family life and childhood as possible, without unnecessary restrictions.*
- *The central importance of the child's relationship with their foster carer should be acknowledged and foster carers should be recognised as core members of the team working with the child.*
- *Foster carers have a right to full information about the child.*
- *It is essential that foster carers receive relevant support services and development opportunities in order to provide the best care for children.*
- *Genuine partnership between all those involved in fostering children is essential for the NMS to deliver the best outcomes for children; this includes the Government, local government, other statutory agencies, fostering service providers and foster carers.*

(Department for Education, 2011, pp. 3–4)

From these values come themes that recur throughout this handbook:

- Good foster care treats every child or young person as an individual and practice centres on meeting their particular individual needs.
- A successful adult life is based on good parenting and a broad range of experiences and opportunities, including education.
- The role of foster carers is given central importance. Your relationship with the child or young person is crucial. Carers should act as any good parent would towards their own child.

- Foster care is a partnership and carers are not alone. You should receive help, support and training. You should be respected and listened to as part of the team around the child and given full information about the child.

Fostering Regulations: what they mean for you

Regulation 16 specifies the duties of the fostering service regarding education, employment and leisure activities.

Education is identified as being of crucial significance in a child's life. The service and all foster carers should promote the educational achievement of children.

Education has a wide definition, going beyond learning at school to incorporate leisure and social activities, which the service should also promote. This theme – a broad approach to the meaning of education for a child's life – is picked up throughout this book.

You and the fostering service must:

- promote regular school attendance;
- promote children's participation in school activities;
- put in place a procedure to monitor children's educational achievement, progress and school attendance;
- provide foster carers with what you need to meet the educational needs of children living with you, including information, assistance and equipment.

School attendance is of primary importance and the service must know how well a child is doing at any given time. This may sound obvious but experience suggests that basic information like this is not always readily available for all children and young people. Without such knowledge, it is harder to be proactive and nip problems in the bud, or, for example, to understand how a child is feeling about school. Is he missing certain days because he doesn't like a particular lesson or is he being bullied, for example? It is easy for problems to slip through cracks or to miss patterns of non-attendance.

Note that the fostering service will provide this system of monitoring progress and attendance; you don't have to create it.

The child must be enabled to take part in school activities. Education is therefore seen as going beyond the classroom. It includes encouraging the child to make friends and be part of the school community. Extra-curricular activities are also good for developing self-esteem and confidence. They help children settle in a new school if they have had to move or when they transfer from primary to secondary school.

You can also encourage children to be involved in any decisions taken about their own lives, for instance by talking to them about their preferences to help them choose which activities they would like to take part in.

These two foster carers from the North West and West Midlands speak from experience:

> Cathryn: *You can't force them to do things, you just have to give them choices and let them decide what they would like to do.*
>
> Alison: *Encourage them to try lots of things and find their own way. It could be that they like swimming, bikes or horse riding – it really depends on the child. You need to tailor your activities to the individual.*
>
> (https://perpetualfostering.co.uk/insights/101-foster-care-tips-encouraging-hobbies-interests/)

Meeting a child's broad educational needs requires a partnership with the fostering service and carer working together on the child's behalf. Regulation 16 also uses the phrase 'as may be necessary to meet the educational needs' – an approach based on the needs of each individual child and young person.

The Regulation goes on to address the needs of children of school age but who are not attending mainstream school. If the service provides education for such children, it must be suitable, taking account of their age, ability, aptitude and special educational needs (SEN).

Finally, where a young person is above compulsory school age, the fostering service must help with arrangements for education, training and employment. This forms a link between education and adulthood. Duties go beyond the school and support must be offered to the young person as he makes choices about his future. This includes further training, help finding and keeping a job and support into further education, including university (see Chapter 10).

National Minimum Standards: Standard 8

NMS 8.1: Children, including pre-school children and older children, have a foster home that promotes a learning environment and supports their development.

Here the value of the foster home in helping a child or young person achieve their potential and do well in education is recognised. You must encourage your child to learn using age- and ability-appropriate language and materials, and to see that education has value, now and in adulthood.

> *The home is the single most significant environmental factor in enabling children to develop the trust, attitude and skills that will help them to learn and engage positively with the world. A good home learning environment provides the love, security, stimulation, encouragement and opportunities that help children to flourish.*
>
> (Roberts, 2009)

A positive learning environment is created when children are listened to, responded to, talked to, respected and valued as individuals.

Language

The most effective interactions between parents and children incorporate:

- talking generally – using a wide vocabulary;
- praise and acceptance;
- using language with a high information content;
- giving children choices;
- listening to children and responding;
- doing things together.

The language used and the activities chosen vary according to the age and ability of the child but the principles are the same whether for babies or teenagers.

Reading stories, reading together, listening to audiobooks, playing with letters and numbers, drawing and painting together – these and other similar activities develop relationships as well as learning skills, conveying a strong message to your child that you will make one-to-one time for him (see Chapter 7).

Learning and the carer as a role model

The child or young person picks up cues from their carers. Children will be encouraged to read if they see you reading too. Help them with homework, and maybe do some quiet activities during their homework time. Respond to their interests – listen attentively, suggest websites or buying a book to follow up; research it yourself so you can develop your future conversations.

Nobody expects carers to know everything. What's important is your enthusiasm for what children and young people are doing and being positive about their thoughts and their opinions.

Birth children in fostering families are looked up to by fostered children. They can talk about school, how to manage, how they are looking ahead to adulthood and how education plays a part in their plans. Birth children often have excellent strategies, for example, for managing homework and problems in school. Encourage them to share. Learning is fun!

NMS 8.2: Children have access to a range of educational resources to support their learning and have opportunities beyond the school day to engage in activities that promote learning.

Useful resources include:

- play;
- libraries;
- buying books;
- reading together;
- making things, art and craft;
- computer games and the internet;
- looking at nature.

The internet is full of educational resources, e.g. simple games to involve children in maths, English, problem-solving, etc. Schools will be able to point you in the right direction, e.g. sites that support classroom learning with age- and ability-appropriate material (see list of resources towards the end of this book).

It may sound obvious, but other people are resources too. Friends and family or the child's friends will have expertise and enthusiasm to share, to make learning fun and involve children and young people in activities.

Note that "learning" and "opportunities" are defined broadly. Here is the space for you to use your ideas and creativity. Consider experiential learning, following up a child's interests, joining local clubs to pursue activities, encourage sports, music and other pursuits where he can be part of the community. This develops confidence and self-esteem. Children and young people who feel good about themselves have a good chance of developing their potential.

NMS 8.3: Children are supported to attend school, or alternative provision, regularly.

Regular attendance is of primary importance. There are several inter-related expectations here.

Travel to and from school

You should make arrangements appropriate for the child's age and abilities, ensuring that he is safe on the journey. Younger children should be taken to and from school. Some children and young people with a disability will have transport provided for them by the local authority. It will organise this transport and pay for it. Generally though, local authorities expect foster carers to transport children to school if it is within 20 miles of the foster home. Any changes to the regular transport arrangements must go through the social worker. For older children and young people, judge their ability to do the journey on their own. It's a big step in their development, as in the following foster carer's account:

> *Safety and risk were big worries for me. Gradually, I let her out unsupervised – first to play in the close, then to the corner shop 100 yards away. I say "unsupervised" – that's what she thought but I kept an eye on her all the way! She didn't see me! Felt a bit sneaky but there you go. Secondary school*

was about a mile away. All her mates went on the bus. So I worked towards making the journey safe and familiar. We did it together, broke it down into stages – walked to the bus stop, got on the bus, got the money ready. Then she did bits of the journey on her own. Now she does it all. I watch her onto the bus and I have this app with the bus arrival times, so if she says she missed a bus I know if she's telling the truth or not. It's done her a power of good, she's much more confident now.

Another carer voices similar concerns:

With my own kids, I let them go to after-school clubs, or a friend picked them up after school. For these two, I always take and collect them personally. I think it reassures them. They've been with me for months now but they still need reminding of our routine, that I will be there for them when I promise I will.

Make sure he has everything he needs for school

- uniform;
- kit for the day's timetable, e.g. gym or sport;
- equipment;
- any consent forms for activities;
- appropriate financial support for trips and after school activities;
- completed homework;
- his planner, if at secondary school – make sure you read and sign it when required.

Dig around in the bottom of his bag for notes! Check online too – many schools communicate with parents via email and/or the school site.

Is there anything stopping the child from going to school?

Be proactive – sense if there is reluctance on the child's part to go to school, try to find out what that might be and take action accordingly, e.g. support him if he is not confident, advocate on his behalf with the school. Try to nip these problems in the bud before they become a big issue, overwhelming the child. This foster carer's swift action and understanding show how small things can make a big difference:

This teacher, right, I shouldn't say this but she was a bit old-fashioned, like the teachers I had when I was a girl and that was a long time ago, believe me. She expected kids to have a pen and ruler with them, other things, rubber, you know. She got angry with kids if they didn't have them. It's all about Standards, I suppose. Anyway, my little one was upset about going to school for a week or so. Turns out she was worried the teacher would have a go at her. I made sure she had all her stuff, we put it in her bag every morning before she left so she knew it was there. Little thing really, made a big difference to her. Funny what's on their minds isn't it?

NMS 8.4: Children are helped by their foster carer to achieve their educational or training goals and foster carers are supported to work with a child's education provider to maximise each child's achievement and to minimise any underachievement.

Three main expectations come together here. The first is that you must help the child or young person understand their goals. This depends on their capabilities. It could be going for qualifications or a university place; it could be 100 per cent attendance or taking part in a particular school activity. For young people, it could be work-based training or finding an apprenticeship. Strike a balance between being realistic, or else he could be set up to fail, and encourage him to aim high, to be the very best he can be.

This goes hand in hand with working closely with the school, college or workplace to help the child or young person achieve. As above, this implies an active and positive attitude towards promoting achievement. Other sections of this handbook discuss ways of working alongside educational professionals, advocating on behalf of children and young people and knowing who's who in the school.

Thirdly, note the phrasing here: 'foster carers are supported...' The fostering service should offer support, advice and resources to assist the carer in their work.

NMS 8.5: The fostering service has, and is fully implementing, a written education policy that promotes and values children's education and is understood by foster carers.

This section is primarily aimed at the fostering service, which should prepare a policy and procedure aimed at fulfilling the expectations contained in the

Standards. You should know what they contain as it relates to your duties. A good policy specifies what carers must do in order to fulfil their role in respect of a child or young person's education.

Note that the service is obliged to make sure that carers know about the policy and understand the expectations and duties it confers. Carers may be asked to sign a document to confirm they have read and understood it; it will be discussed in supervision with SSWs and monitored via the annual Foster Carer Review.

NMS 8.6: Foster carers maintain regular contact with each child's school and other education settings, attending all parents' meetings as appropriate and advocating for the child where appropriate.

This makes explicit the expectation already outlined in several points above, namely, that you should create and maintain a relationship with schools and colleges, and advocate on the child's behalf where necessary. Parents' meetings are not optional – you *must* attend. Depending on the child or young person's care plan, the birth parent may go as well. If so, talk this through with your SSW. It shows the parent that you are working together with them on behalf of their child, and it shows the child that you and the parent are working together on his behalf too.

NMS 8.7: Foster carers engage and work with schools, colleges and other organisations to support children's education, including advocating to help overcome any problems the child may be experiencing in their education setting. Foster carers have up-to-date information about each child's educational progress and school attendance record.

The first part of this Standard reinforces the approach we have discussed already, namely actively promoting a relationship with the educational setting and advocating on a child or young person's behalf. Once more, it shows the key role of the foster carer in helping children and young people to achieve.

Also, you must keep up to date with how the child or young person is doing, including their attendance. Most schools have a system to report unauthorised absences on the day but if in doubt, check regularly. Progress can be monitored through reports, a home-school record book, parents' evenings or simply a call to the teacher.

Other relevant Standards

The NMS cover the expectations of the fostering service and their carers in some detail. In addition to Standard 8 outlined above, NMS 1–4 are noteworthy and relevant to education.

NMS 1 is related to 'the child's wishes and feelings and the views of those significant to them'.

This Standard requires that:

- Children's views, wishes and feelings are acted upon unless this is contrary to their interests or adversely affects other household members.
- Children understand how their views have been taken into account.

These statements apply to all aspects of foster care. In respect of education, foster carers need to understand the child or young person's views about his education, including his aspirations and any school-related problems, and be able to share this on his behalf with the team around the child, or at meetings. For example, establish how he would like to refer to you, e.g. as "auntie" or "uncle", and make sure that his teachers are aware of this.

In addition, the child or young person must know that you recognise his acute awareness of his care status. Reflect back to him that you understand, respond to any changes he may seek, and explain how his wishes are being acted upon, including the reasons why you may not be following these.

NMS 1.5 states that children have the right to independent advice and support, a further avenue for the child's voice to be heard.

Your fostering service and the child's social worker will have details of organisations able to offer this. For example, Fosterline, the National Youth Advocacy Service (NYAS) and CoramVoice each provide advocacy and advice for looked after children and care leavers (see Useful Resources section for details).

NMS 2 requires carers to promote a positive identity, potential and value diversity through individualised care.

While education is not explicitly mentioned, it places strong emphasis on foster carers' role in enabling children and young people to develop as rounded individuals – emotionally resilient, self-confident and with a positive self-view.

NMS 3 is headed 'Promoting positive behaviour and relationships'.

Relevant to education in particular are:

- Foster carers have high expectations of all the foster children in their household.
- Carers promote, model and support positive behaviour.
- Carers help children develop skills to build and maintain positive relationships and resolve conflicts.
- Carers support children when they encounter discrimination or bullying.

Note also the requirement for the fostering service to ensure that you have full information about the child or young person in your care and to pursue shortfalls with the local authority (NMS 3.9). Carers often say that they have not been kept up to date or given the information they need to provide the best possible care.

NMS 4 covers safeguarding and the need to make children safe and feel safe.

Note the inclusion in NMS 4.4 of 'foster carers encourage children to take appropriate risks as a normal part of growing up'. Foster carers should treat children and make decisions like any reasonable parent. Caring for foster children and young people is not about wrapping them up in cotton wool, it is about giving them the skills and self-esteem to manage risks and to gradually take more responsibility as they grow up. Your role is to set the parameters for this depending on the situation and your understanding of the age and ability of the child or young person.

Key points

- Whereas the Regulations stipulate broad duties, the NMS provide a more detailed account of what is required of foster carers.
- The Regulations and value statement give fostering a purpose. It is not a temporary fix nor a holding operation until the young person turns 18. It is about preparing him for a successful adulthood, about giving him a chance to achieve, to fulfil his ambitions; a chance to amaze, to be the person he wants to be. These are lofty, laudable ambitions. Foster care is important and you are fundamental to these achievements.
- Every child is an individual with potential. Your role is to help him identify and fulfil that potential.
- Carers often say they see a child progress in small steps; it's gradual, but every achievement, however small, is valuable. For some, it could be straight As and a university place; for others, it's going from the door to the school bus on their own. Both are equally valuable for that individual child.

3 Planning and the team around the child

This book often mentions the "team around the child" and the role of foster carers in advocating for her. We follow with examples of how you can make this work. You can't tell teachers what to do but you can help them better understand the particular needs of your child and work with them to put that understanding to good use in the classroom. The insights in Chapter 1 about the effect of deficient early life experiences on attachment patterns are translated into practical suggestions for managing behaviour and helping learning. Think about how these and other strategies might be a good fit for your child. Work alongside the teachers to put them into action. Perhaps adapt some of them for your home; after all, you are dealing with the same attachment issues. Continuity between home and school makes children and young people feel secure.

This chapter aims to enable you:

- to understand what it is expected of you as a foster carer in relation to your child's education;
- to learn how to play a full part in the planning process;
- to meet the needs of the child and young person in your care.

Think of this as a map to steer you through the maze of duties and expectations. You can refer to it in order to know what is happening at every stage of the planning process for the child or young person, so that you can make the most of your contribution.

The care planning framework should be familiar to carers from their preparation to foster and subsequent training and experience. The emphasis here is on planning the child's education. Three key roles are covered, incorporating the social worker, Independent Reviewing Officer (IRO) and supervising social worker (SSW).

Decision-making: roles and responsibilities

The child's social worker

The child or young person's social worker is responsible for ensuring that her welfare is safeguarded and promoted, and for the implementation of the Care Plan set in place to meet her needs. This includes making sure she is safe and well cared for, receives good health care and is appropriately educated. It is essential that her educational arrangements are discussed with both her social worker and the SSW before the placement starts.

The children's social worker is expected to:

- visit the child or young person;
- provide all the information you need to care for her;
- invite you to meetings;
- give you key information in writing, e.g. about contact arrangements, legal orders;
- create and maintain the placement plan (see below).

He or she is also responsible for putting into practice all major decisions about a child or young person's education. If you are in any doubt about any course of action, check first with the children's social worker, either directly or via your SSW.

As simplistic as this may sound, the single most valuable piece of advice for any carer who might be worried or unsure about what to do is 'When in doubt, ask!' Remember that your fostering service and SSW can advise you too, but they cannot take a decision if, for example, certain consents are required or a significant change in education provision is being contemplated.

The children's social worker acts on behalf of the children's services department of the local authority that placed the child or young person in the foster home. She or he will consult the manager of their team and has access to a range of other sources of advice, such as a specialist legal department. They also take into account local authority policy, including finance and available resources. Some decisions are taken at a higher level, i.e. by a more senior manager.

Decisions at any level should relate to the child or young person's Care Plan and the social worker should look to that plan when it comes to deciding any course of action.

The Independent Reviewing Officer

The IRO is an independent person charged with overseeing the creation and implementation of the child or young person's care plan.

The three key elements of their role are:

1. chairing the child or young person's review – to which you will be invited;
2. establishing a plan to meet the assessed needs of the child or young person;
3. monitoring the implementation of the care plan and Review decisions – they make sure that everyone has completed their agreed tasks, evaluate progress and re-plan if necessary.

The IRO's role is fundamental in child care planning. They are expected to:

- make sure the care plan is based on an accurate and up-to-date assessment of the child or young person's needs;
- understand the child or young person's wishes and feelings and incorporate them into the plans – to this end, the IRO meets with them before every review;
- ensure all relevant evidence and views are incorporated into the plans;
- allocate specific tasks, with timescales, to all participants, including the children's social worker, carers and the fostering service;
- ensure that all resources necessary to meet the child or young person's needs are available;
- check that tasks have been undertaken and resources provided.

IROs have the power to take any concerns to the local authority. You can contact them directly; you don't have to wait for the next review.

The supervising social worker

Every foster carer must have an SSW responsible for supervision and support. This is provided by your fostering service, whether it be a local authority or independent provider.

Your SSW is generally your first point of contact, the first person you go to if you require any advice and/or for sharing information about the child or young person's well-being. One of the aims of good SSW practice is to establish a professional relationship and open communication with carers to sustain every aspect of their care of the child. This includes support for the practical and emotional needs of the foster carer and their family.

The supervisory aspect of an SSW's duties is to make sure you comply with your responsibilities as a carer to the required standard. In respect of education, these expectations are set out in detail below. These standards are formally reviewed in your annual Foster Carer Review. Again, the manner in which you have promoted educational opportunities and achievement for the children and young people in your care is part of that.

Contact your SSW for advice and support. They will know what the placement plan and care plan contain. They will also know you, your capabilities and experience. Their advice around putting decisions into practice is tailored to this knowledge and understanding.

Understand the different responsibilities of the child's social worker and the SSW in respect of decision-making. The SSW cannot change decisions: that rests with the child or young person's social worker. But they can advise you on how to implement them – for example, how to interpret decisions taken and what they mean for your work – and whether a decision falls within your remit or has to go to the social worker for clarification. If they don't know the answer, they can contact the local authority on your behalf.

This applies equally to liaising with other professionals, including those in education. For instance, the SSW will support you in school meetings and can contact school staff on your behalf and advocate for the child or young person.

The detailed arrangements for decision-making, including education, are agreed in a series of meetings as part of the child care planning process. They are recorded and you must be given a copy.

Care Plan

The Care Plan sets out the plan for the child or young person in the short, medium and long term based on their identified needs and how they will be addressed. This is the key document in respect of child care planning and it is reviewed after three months, then at least every six months after that.

The Personal Education Plan (PEP) forms part of the Care Plan; it comprises a detailed record of education and achievement and is explained at the end of this chapter.

The Placement Plan is also part of the Care Plan and covers in detail the way in which the placement will meet the needs of the child or young person. It gets down to day-to-day detail about every aspect of the child's well-being, including her educational needs, and how you are expected to respond.

Placement Plan

The Placement Plan is the children's social worker's responsibility. They will call a meeting to discuss and agree it either before the child or young person comes to live with you or within five working days of their arrival. You must be invited; in fact, it will probably take place in your home. The child's social worker or her supervisor or manager chairs, and anyone able to make a significant contribution to the discussions and decisions about identifying and meeting the needs of the child or young person is invited. This may also include the birth parents.

The child's wishes and feelings are vital to the planning process and therefore to this meeting. She should not only be invited but also be supported to attend and to share her wishes and aspirations.

As part of the Care Plan, the Placement Plan is reviewed after three months and then every six months, to coincide with the child's review timetable.

Educational needs

CoramBAAF has produced a Placement Plan format, guidance and template for local authorities. The section entitled "Educational needs" stresses how the information provided needs to cover what is known about the child/young person's previous experience of school.

For example:

- *Did they attend regularly?*
- *What did they enjoy/not enjoy about school?*
- *Are there things they find difficult about attending?*

The meeting explores how you are going to encourage and develop the child/young person's learning.

- *Does the school have academic monitoring days? What other opportunities are there to meet with teachers/tutors?*
- *Where is the space for the child/young person to do homework? What are the expectations of the carer to assist the child?*
- *What agreements are there regarding the child/young person having access to and using a computer to assist with homework?*
- *Details of an EHC (Education, Health and Care) plan and provisions need to be clearly set out.*
- *If the child has specific learning needs, are there any services that would be beneficial for the carers to use with the child, e.g. Catch Up (www.catchup.org/).*

Details of transport arrangements:

- *What are the expectations of the foster carer in relation to transporting the child/young person to and from school?*
- *Can the child/young person make their own way to school on public transport? Are there any risks that need to be considered?*
- *Where the foster carer cannot transport the child/young person, are there other options, other than using taxis, which may normalise the child/young person's situation?*
- *What are the arrangements if the child is not in full-time education or is excluded from educational provision?*

(Dibben, 2018, pp. 13–14)

The section concludes by making sure any action points are incorporated into the Care Plan.

The purpose of the Placement Plan is to get everyone to agree on the information required under the above headings. Some of this is a matter of record, e.g. the Statement of Special Needs or Education, Health and Care (EHC) plan as it is now called. Some may be up for discussion, such as delegated authority (see below). The process therefore helps to identify areas of disagreement or a shortfall in provision; participants can then work together to try to resolve the problems. Your contribution is key.

The plan also makes sure you have all the information you need. One of the most common difficulties that carers identify when a child or young person first comes to live with them is a lack of information. The plan addresses this problem directly. The child's background and history are covered elsewhere in the Placement Plan; here it encourages detailed discussion of things like school transport arrangements – fine when they work smoothly but time-consuming and frustrating for foster carers when they don't. The Placement Plan should record the transport arrangements and whom to contact to solve any problems.

Note that the section on education begins with a clear, agreed statement of what the child or young person needs. The term "needs-based" or something similar crops up throughout this book. Here it is, top of the list: needs-based planning in action.

It's also important to realise that this definition of needs is not cut and dried. On the contrary, there may well not be a consensus. It is essential to know this and state it openly. This is the opportunity to have that discussion and try to come to some agreement. Your views are integral to this process.

In all the sections, the Placement Plan should record:

- the child's needs;
- relevant information;
- the arrangements for meeting those needs;
- the foster carer's tasks in meeting those needs;
- action plans – who else is doing what;
- whom to contact if there is a problem.

The Placement Plan documentation also contains a useful table of education-related contacts, with space for the name and contact details of key personnel and information about relevant resources.

Delegated authority

Which decisions can you make about and for the child, i.e. which decisions are "delegated" to the foster carer? This is known as "delegated authority" and comes in the form of an agreement drawn up as part of the Placement Plan. You should be fully involved and will be given a copy, so you know what you can and cannot agree for the child. It is an important part of the process of giving looked after children and young people the same opportunities as their peers and helping them to live a normal childhood. You should be given permission, as far as possible, to make commonsense everyday decisions in family life and to act as a responsible parent would towards their own children. Where decisions around consent do not rest with the foster carer, this should be recorded clearly and you must stick to this.

The education section includes:

- signing consent for school trips;
- consent for school photos;
- consent for school activities.

Other sections cover consent for issues such as sleepovers, joining leisure activities and outings, all part of helping the child or young person make friends at school and in the community.

This foster carer's account shows how easy it is for consent to be overlooked:

> *The school were doing this thing about a school garden and J was really looking forward to it. He and my husband were always pottering about in our garden. Funny really, he's always top speed about everything, but with the garden he sits quietly and chats. Anyway, I get to school on the morning and overhear the secretary talking about it to other parents, says the local paper's coming down, photographer, you know. I said hang on. Didn't want to say much in front of people in the playground but told his class teacher what was what. Rang my supervising social worker in a flap, she said she would call social services. They wouldn't agree without talking about it some*

more, so that's that. I get it, and it's good to hear from you that I did the right thing but I felt really bad for him. My worker's going to bring it up at his review in a couple of weeks.

Legal status

If the child or young person is on a full care order, the local authority holds the decisive weight of decision-making responsibility and makes decisions as would a parent.

On major decisions, they would first consult with the parent, defined as someone with parental responsibility, unless for whatever reason this has been prohibited by the court, or it is not safe for the child or young person to do so. They will also inform the family of any changes in the child or young person's education.

Every situation is different, but as an example, if the family has some ongoing contact with a child or young person, the local authority may seek the family's views if it contemplated moving her from mainstream schooling to special education, but not if she had changed sets in the classroom. However, it would keep the family up to date with educational progress via the child's review.

If the child or young person is subject to an interim care order, the authority would consult with the family about major decisions, keep them informed and inform the court, who would consider any disagreements and, if necessary, rule on them.

If the child or young person is accommodated, i.e. the parent has agreed to her being looked after under section 20 of the 1989 Children Act, the parent retains decision-making responsibilities. They must be consulted and their wishes acted upon. This would include, in addition to all the examples above, seeking their permission for the child to have a haircut or going on a school trip. As a carer, you cannot sign the permission slip without the delegated authority to do so.

Personal Education Plans (PEPs)

All looked after children must have a PEP. This forms an integral part of the child or young person's Care Plan, a statutory requirement that covers all aspects of their safety, well-being and development.

Its purpose is to 'support the personalised learning of the child' (Department for Education, 2014b, p. 32). As such, it brings together the recurrent themes of this guide, namely:

- needs-based education planning with shared goals to ensure a child or young person achieves their full potential;
- establishing and maintaining the link between home and school;
- involving everyone who can support a child or young person's progress;
- enabling the child or young person to participate;
- ensuring the child or young person has the resources they need to achieve their potential.

What's in the PEP?

The PEP covers all aspects of a child or young person's educational development. This is broadly defined to include her relationships with peers and leisure activities.

It must contain the following information:

1. The child's educational and training history, including:
    - schools attended;
    - attendance and conduct record;
    - achievements – academic and others;
    - any special educational needs.
2. existing arrangements for education, including any special education provision or provision to promote educational achievement;
3. planned changes to the existing arrangements, including provision to minimise any disruption;
4. leisure interests;
5. the role of people caring for the child in promoting educational achievements and leisure interests.

This information is assembled for the first meeting and forms the basis of the Core Document. This creates a record of the child or young person's history that stays with them wherever they are living and going to school, and which the social worker updates after every meeting.

The PEP is then made up of the Core Document, the school year group review form containing information about attendance and progress (supplied by the school), and a form seeking the views of the child or young person.

It is part of a process of ongoing support for educational attainment. There is a strong and welcome emphasis on identifying short- and long-term targets, and planning intervention strategies to achieve them. In other words, if the child or young person is falling behind in any way, this should be identified and steps taken to address the problem.

Each PEP gives details of the tasks required to put the plan into action, including who will complete each of those tasks, and specifies timescales. The updated PEP makes sure these tasks have been completed, evaluates how well the plans have been achieved and re-plans if necessary.

The designated teacher (explained in the next chapter) leads on how the PEP is developed and used in school to make sure the child's progress towards education targets is monitored. The virtual school head (VSH) takes an overview and quality assurance role on the understanding that the PEP should:

> *... be a "living", evolving, comprehensive and enduring record of the child's experience, progress and achievement (academic and otherwise), and inform any discussion about education during statutory reviews of the child's wider care plan.*
>
> (Department for Education, 2018, para 25)

The carer and child or young person must have a copy of the up-to-date PEP.

The child's social worker cannot take significant decisions about a child or young person's education without reviewing the PEP. (A useful guide to what goes into a PEP can be found at http://leedschildcare.proceduresonline.com/pdfs/how_to_write_pep.pdf.)

Timescales

A PEP must be developed within 20 working days of the child or young person becoming looked after.

Timescales are dictated by the care planning timetable, the duties contained in the Care Planning Placement and Case Review Regulations (England) 2010. The PEP must be available for the first review of the Care Plan, which again takes place within 20 working days of the child or young person becoming looked after. Therefore, the first PEP may actually be ready before the usually quoted 20-day limit in order to be available for the review.

If a child or young person is placed in an emergency, the PEP must be initiated within 10 working days (Department for Education, 2018, para 23).

Subsequently, the PEP should be reviewed every school term. This is a minimum number – it can be more often if required. A PEP review should also take place if a child changes school.

Note: Carers and social workers should be aware of an apparent discrepancy. Local authority policies and procedures typically state that PEPs should be reviewed every six months. This fits with the timetable for looked after children reviews. However, the Statutory Guidance states that 'VSHs should make arrangements for PEPs to be reviewed each school term' (as above, para 28) – in other words, three times a year.

Note also that the child's social worker is responsible for arranging for the PEP to be reviewed whereas the Statutory Guidance talks of the virtual school head arranging the PEP review. In practice, it may be that the authorities call a PEP meeting every six months and the VSH reviews it termly without necessarily calling a full meeting. (You will find more on the role of the VSH in the next chapter.)

For busy foster carers, this may seem an insignificant point. However, many carers bemoan the lack of properly constituted educational planning; ensuring that termly meetings to encourage progress is monitored and actions are current is an important part of helping the child or young person achieve in education.

Meetings should take place during the school day at a time that is convenient for every participant, including the carer and the child or young person.

Given their central importance in planning a child or young person's future, the timing of the PEP should take into account the stages of her education. For example, the transition to secondary school requires detailed consideration. A PEP early in Year 6 sets the goals and establishes the support needed to help the child achieve Key Stage 2 targets and plan for secondary school applications. Meetings in the following two terms should monitor progress, assess if extra resources are required and plan the move to secondary school. Similarly, meeting early in Year 11 sets plans and resources in place for the GCSE timetable.

Arranging the PEP

The responsibility for initiating the PEP lies with the child's social worker. They must consult with the VSH and the designated teacher.

The meeting must include the child's social worker, the foster carer, the child or young person and the designated teacher.

The child's family should be invited if appropriate, either the parents or perhaps grandparents if they are heavily involved in the child's life. Any other professionals with a role to play in the child or young person's education, now or in the future, should also be invited.

Preparation

The child's social worker prepares an agenda, alongside the VSH or the designated teacher. This should be circulated in advance.

Good preparation is essential. Participants should be ready to produce relevant information and evidence. It is not a task of the meeting to ask for this information to be gathered, rather it is the responsibility of participants to have it to hand to facilitate the making of the best possible future plans. For instance, the school should share attendance figures, grades/achievement levels, subject options and reports from individual teachers.

Foster carers play a vital role here in two respects. You know the child or young person well. Day to day, you prepare her for school, support her with homework, understand her attitudes and approach. You know what she enjoys and what stresses she experiences. It is crucial that the meeting takes this into account.

In addition, you are usually best placed to enable the child or young person to participate fully. Meetings are difficult for children and young people, so you can explain what the meeting is about and who will be there. Help her say what she wishes to say. This may entail exploring what she wants from education, thinking about her future and her aspirations. Perhaps the child or young person might make some notes in advance, write down the five key things she wants to say. Above all, you can give them the confidence to be part of the decision-making about their own lives. This foster carer recounts a very positive experience, both for her and the girl in her care:

> *Before she came to live with us, Julie hated school. Always rowing with teachers and kids. With us, she settled a bit, so we persuaded her in the end to come to the PEP and the parents' evening, which happened on the same day. She said no way for ages, but we said we would be with her all the time. She heard how well she was doing and that the teachers were very pleased with how hard she was trying. Went in, eyes on the floor, wouldn't look at anyone. Walked out floating on air. And if I'm honest, so were we!*

There is no set guidance as to who chairs the meeting. However, the social worker is usually best placed to do so. It is important for participants to be aware of who the Chair is and who has responsibility for putting decisions into practice.

School communication and reviews

Attendance

It is important for your child to have good attendance at school in order to make progress. You will normally receive support initially from her school and later her social worker if you are experiencing difficulties getting her to attend.

Your child might miss school if she is too ill to go in or if you have permission from the school for the absence. If she has a health problem and is unable to attend for a long period of time, support is available from www.gov.uk/illness-child-education.

Holidays

You must gain permission from the head teacher if you want to take your child out of school during term time. You need to apply to him or her in advance and you can be fined if you take a child out of school without permission. Looked after children often miss school when transferring placement and this can affect progress (for more information see www.gov.uk/education-attendance-council).

School uniform

Each school decides what its uniform will be and will have a policy on this. School uniform has many benefits with all children attending in similar clothing and creating a sense of belonging. Children can be disciplined if the correct uniform is not worn. This may result in a detention or being sent home to change. In extreme cases, where there is a constant repetition of incorrect uniform being worn, this can lead to exclusion.

What is a home–school agreement?

Most secondary schools have a home–school agreement to be signed by the school, the parent/carer and the child. This will include elements such as being respectful to one other, attending on time and following school rules. They are the expectations that each person should have of the other. If your child is finding it difficult to follow school rules, then seek support and ask for a discussion with a member of staff, such as the class teacher, form tutor or head of year.

Parent/carer evenings

Parent/carer evenings are a time to discuss the progress your child has been making and to view her work. It is a time for sharing and celebrating the things that are going well, as well as discussing areas that could be improved.

In primary schools, you will meet your child's class teacher to discuss school work and your child may show you work of which she is most proud. If she has special educational needs, there may have to be an additional review meeting where more specific details are discussed regarding targets and progress.

In secondary schools, you will normally book appointments with individual subject teachers. This can feel a bit busy and chaotic at times, with some hanging around and appointments running late. Be prepared and have plenty of time so that you can build a picture of your child's progress.

School reviews

Different reviews take place within a school. We have discussed the PEP and subsequent reviews; in addition, if your child has a special educational need, they are likely to have a further review. Previously these were called school action or school action plus reviews, but they are now named a one-plan review. You will meet with your child's special educational needs co-ordinator (SENCO) (see Chapter 4) and class teacher once a term and discuss her progress against set targets. You will also discuss any reports that have been sought from specialists who have been working with her, such as a speech and language therapist. If your child is receiving any additional support in school, such as attending a nurture group or as part of an intervention group, then this will be reviewed to see how effective it is.

If your child has an EHC plan (see Chapter 9), this will be reviewed annually with a member of a specialist team from the local authority.

Key points

- Fostering is a partnership between carers and the fostering service. They must support you in order to achieve on behalf of children. If they don't, you should share this with them and resolve problems so you can move forward.
- PEPs don't have to be just another meeting in the diary. They are an opportunity to get everyone together with the child or young person to talk about a vital element of their lives – their educational attainment.
- Teachers are busy people. PEP meetings usually take place in schools, so it's a perfect chance to gather staff with a role to play. Use them to problem-solve. If communication between you and the school is a problem, get everyone together to communicate face to face. The same goes for any hiccups with communication between school staff with different responsibilities.
- Check with the social worker in advance of the PEP to see who is coming, suggest other possible invitees and put forward things you want to talk

about as agenda items. Your SSW can do this for you if you prefer. You hold the child's story. Make sure everyone else knows that story too.

- You know what works for your child. Be ready to share all this and if you think the meeting is not responding, be ready to say it again. Your SSW will support you. Talk to the child a day or two before the meeting. Work out with her what she wants to say. Perhaps write down a few short points. She might want to write something and give it to everyone, with your help of course. Perhaps she would prefer if you spoke up for her.
- This is not just about education. It is about building trust and strengthening relationships. It shows the child that you and other adults in their lives listen to them and respond to their wishes. Hopefully, by taking part, they feel they have some control over decisions about their lives.

4 The school system: roles and responsibilities

This chapter explains the roles and responsibilities of school personnel in respect of children in foster care. As with any organisation, carers need to understand how the system works so they can better support the child or young person's education.

This can be complex, involving several professionals with overlapping responsibilities. Children's needs can easily become lost in the system so it is important that you know:

- who does what;
- who takes decisions about what;
- with whom to communicate.

First, it helps to understand the role of the virtual school and the virtual school head.

The virtual school head

Every local authority must appoint an officer to ensure they discharge their duty to promote the educational achievement of their looked after children. This is the virtual school head or VSH. Some authorities use a different name such as lead commissioner or head of achievement for children in care, but the role is the same.

A VSH is an experienced teacher with specialist knowledge in relevant areas who provides support to schools and designated teachers. They also work alongside other agencies to promote educational achievement.

Sarah Rivers, VSH for Staffordshire County Council, explains her role:

> *My role is to champion the education of every child and young person who is looked after by the authority I work for, from the age of 0 to 18.*[1] *Today this involves 1,099 children in care. My role follows and supports children wherever they are being educated: in early years settings, mainstream schools, special schools, independent schools, residential schools, colleges, youth offending institutions, hospital, secure children's homes, pupil referral units, alternative education providers and, for the first time this year, boarding schools.*
>
> (Rivers, 2018, p. 153)

While children and young people attend their own school in the usual way, they are also on a "virtual school" roll overseen by the VSH. This comprises all the looked after children for whom the authority is responsible, wherever they live or are educated. Authorities are required to place them either in their home area or as near as possible. However, many live outside their home authority and attend different types of educational establishments. To make sure that every child has the best possible opportunities and that no one becomes lost in the system, the virtual school roll maintains a focus on their needs, and the VSH is charged with obtaining up-to-date information regarding their progress, attendance and achievements.

The local authority must give the VSH sufficient resources to discharge their considerable responsibilities and do their job properly. This includes holding the Pupil Premium budget and allocating money to schools for tutoring, computer hardware, etc.

Each will have a different structure, but usually they will be supported by a team of other educational professionals. This team is called the virtual school.

The VSH has seven core areas of responsibility:

1. knowing who is on the virtual school roll at any given time;

---

1 While the general age for leaving care has now been raised (from 16) to 18, there is growing recognition that many young people need the option of staying with their foster carers at least up to the age of 21, especially given that, in 2019, among the general population the average age for leaving home is 24."Staying put" legislation, endorsed by government and formalised in the Children and Families Act 2014, brought with it extra funding and a commitment to support care who remain in education or training up until their 25th birthday.

2. knowing where they live and where they go to school;
3. monitoring progress and knowing how well they are doing at any given time;
4. establishing and implementing a plan to take action if they are not doing as well as they are capable;
5. being able to evaluate the impact of this plan and actions;
6. understanding their role, accountability and being available for inspection;
7. allocation of the Pupil Premium Plus (PPP) (see following page).

(Department for Education, 2018)

The VSH and foster carers

The VSH plays an essential part in ensuring that the child or young person in foster care receives the best possible service according to his needs. They carry considerable weight in their authorities with a specific remit to improve the educational opportunities available for looked after children.

They enable access to new resources; they may have resources available within the virtual school. They can also advocate powerfully on behalf of the child or young person to ensure that the authority where he lives and goes to school provides everything that he is entitled to.

When a child lives outside his home authority, sometimes carers experience problems with educational provision, ranging from extra help in the classroom through to finding a suitable school place. This should not happen but it does. The VSH has no such boundaries. They are responsible for the child wherever he lives; they unblock logjams, so they must be involved at the earliest possible opportunity to resolve problems.

The VSH advises and supports schools. For example, they work alongside the designated teacher to ensure that the right provision is offered or to ensure your child's needs are understood fully. They can work with carers to encourage the school to implement strategies for dealing with educational or behavioural issues. They sometimes attend PEP meetings and reviews for your child. Their role is multidisciplinary, working with other professions and retaining the child-centred focus.

Pupil Premium Plus (PPP)

The virtual school is also involved in the allocation of the PPP – additional funding paid to schools to raise the attainment of looked after children and young people by providing additional resources according to need. Following the establishment of the Pupil Premium two years earlier, the enhanced PPP was introduced by the Department for Education in 2013 with the aim of closing the attainment gap between looked after and previously looked after children and their peers. Schools are given funds for each child and are accountable for how they use it and how it helps the progress of the child concerned. In 2018–2019 the annual sum allocated per pupil is £2,300. This can be used on any educational resource; in other words, it is closely linked to individual need. It could be used to buy an item to improve learning or to fund extra help or an activity. Examples include:

- individual and small group tuition in English and maths;
- intensive support;
- speech and language support;
- breakfast and support session by a learning mentor;
- laptops to support learning;
- support for improving attendance;
- music tuition;
- practical work with families;
- a range of educational experiences – trips, residential schools;
- career-linked events.

The school website has a legal requirement to show how the extra money is spent and what it achieves, and this is reviewed by Ofsted. The governors and head teacher have a say in whether any of it can be spent on an individual child as opposed to a general school facility. Foster carers are in a strong position to ask about this as it is their child for whom the premium is being made available.

This foster carer learned that it pays to be persistent:

I know about the Pupil Premium because I'm a governor at another school. E needed extra help with speech and language. He'd been seeing the speech therapist but that stopped. The school said they didn't have the therapist hours available, so I raised this at the PEP, asked why the Pupil Premium couldn't be used. The school looked doubtful, but we got it, sessions for the rest of the school year now. Foster carers don't know about the Pupil Premium always, it's there to pay for those extras. Don't ask don't get.

Designated teachers

Many looked after children and previously looked after children have suffered disrupted learning, many have missed extended periods of school, and many of them have special educational needs (SEN). The gaps in their learning – and in many cases the emotional impact of their experiences – are likely to become significant barriers to their progress. The complexity of this fragmented educational experience needs careful assessment and planning. Excellent practice in supporting looked after and previously looked after children already exists in many schools. The designated teacher role is statutory to help ensure that effective practice becomes universal.

(Department for Education, 2017, Statutory Guidance 1.1)

All schools must appoint a designated teacher with responsibility for looked after children. They play an essential role in promoting their educational achievement. They monitor progress, offer support and liaise with school colleagues on behalf of the child or young person.

The governing body of the school has a statutory duty under the Children and Young Persons Act 2008 to appoint a designated teacher for looked after children with the appropriate qualifications, experience and status, including the seniority to influence school policy. In recognition of the importance of the role, this teacher reports to the governors at least annually and must receive the support and resources, including time, to perform the role effectively.

Schools have some flexibility in carrying out the role, depending, for example, on the school's size and structure and the number of looked after children on roll. The designated teacher's role could overlap with other responsibilities, e.g. the head or deputy head, the SENCO in a primary school, or a year head or teacher with other pastoral responsibilities in a larger or secondary school.

The part played by designated teachers may not seem immediately obvious but it is hoped that, like the foster carer quoted below, you will soon appreciate their value.

> *Honest? You know me, I don't get all this jargon. Why can't they give them simple names so you know what they do? Designated this, virtual that. My granddaughter got virtual reality glasses for Christmas, is that the same? What I do know is, this teacher makes it her business to get to know J. Talks to her if she's upset in school. Helps sort out problems with other teachers. Always happy to talk to me, rang back if she was busy. Wish the social worker did that!*

The role of the designated teacher

For our purposes, it is useful to approach the role of the designated teacher from two different, complementary angles:

- their internal responsibilities within the school to promote the needs of looked after children and young people;
- their external responsibilities: working with the team around the child or young person, including the foster carer, the child's social worker and other professionals, advocating for external resources, forming a relationship with the birth family, as appropriate;

These come together to provide a consistent home/school approach, supported by the right resources based on an accurate assessment of the needs of the child. The designated teacher therefore has a third key area of responsibility – to develop, monitor and maintain the child or young person's PEP.

Responsibilities within the school

The designated teacher is an advocate and champion on behalf of looked after children and the voice of the individual child in school. They promote an awareness of their needs and the need to create a school ethos to address them. As such, they disseminate knowledge and understanding about the particular issues inhibiting the educational achievement of looked after children, including the impact of their early life experiences on their self-esteem and their ability to form relationships with staff and peers, and by their ability to learn.

Everyone in the school should be geared towards meeting the needs of looked after children. The designated teacher leads on enabling teachers and support staff to:

- promote a culture in which looked after children believe they can succeed and to aspire to further and higher education;
- have high expectations and realise children and young people may need extra support to achieve them;
- be aware of the emotional, psychological and social effects of loss and separation from birth families;
- understand that children may find it difficult to build relationships with peers and adults;
- understand the child care system, including the foster carer's role.

The school must establish policies and procedures to support this approach. These are linked to other policies, e.g. admissions policies where looked after children are a priority when it comes to applying for a school place, and equality and diversity policies.

Also, the designated teacher will advocate on behalf of children and young people regarding any issues they face, e.g. extra resources to meet their identified learning needs, dispute resolution, bullying and discrimination. They lead on implementing the child's PEP and monitor the progress of every child or young person.

External responsibilities

The designated teacher also plays a valuable outward-facing role in ensuring there are positive and effective channels of communication and partnership working to enable children and young people to make the most of their education. This aspect of their work includes:

- liaising with foster carers around the needs of individual children and young people;
- liaising with social workers and other professionals;

- working with the VSH;
- ensuring that there is a central point of contact in the school (often but not necessarily the designated teacher) to engage with those outside the school.

The designated teacher should be involved in any discussions relating to possible exclusion, and make sure that foster carers and the child's social worker are involved in decision-making.

The designated safeguarding officer

The designated safeguarding officer (or lead) is a named senior teacher with responsibility for safeguarding and child protection in the school, both day to day and in terms of implementing policy and good practice.

They are often called "the designated teacher for safeguarding"; this book uses "designated person" from the legislation to distinguish the role from that of "designated teacher", i.e. "designated teacher for looked after children".

Key elements of their role are:

- ensuring that staff are aware of and understand safeguarding policy and procedure;
- ensuring that they know to whom and how to raise safeguarding concerns;
- raising awareness of signs and symptoms of child abuse and neglect;
- making referrals to children's services;
- monitoring children who have a child protection plan.

Teachers

In primary school, each class has a main teacher who teaches a large range of subjects. This is likely to be your first point of contact and she or he will probably get to know you and your child very well. Some primary schools employ specialist teachers to teach a subject such as PE or music.

In secondary school, your child will meet a large number of teachers each week as they each have specialist subject knowledge. If you need to speak to a teacher about your child's progress, it is best to contact them by phoning the school and arranging a time when they would be free to talk to you.

Tutors

Tutors are teachers in secondary schools with specific responsibility for a tutor or form group. They meet with the group for morning registration and sometimes at other times. Groupings are usually around pupils in the same academic year. Some schools have a mixed age range to help children and young people to integrate, with older pupils offering informal support and guidance.

The tutor's role includes enabling the child or young person to participate fully in the school and to address barriers to learning. They are therefore a useful contact if carers need to approach the school about any problems.

Learning support assistants

The learning support assistant, also known as classroom or teaching assistant, works with pupils in the classroom to support their learning. They may work one-to-one or with groups. An example of their role is to offer extra support for a child or young person with a learning difficulty, thereby enabling them to participate in mainstream class. The nature and extent of that support depends on the child or young person's needs.

School administrative staff

School secretaries play an essential and vibrant part in the organisation of any school, especially at primary level where schools tend to be smaller. They are usually the first point of contact. In primary schools, they administer records around attendance, lateness, absence, etc. They keep on top of the school calendar so they know what events are taking place, and sometimes children who are out of class or ill will gravitate to the school office and the private admin area.

In terms of attendance, many schools now have an automated system to monitor absence and phone you if an absence is unauthorised. It is essential that you respond, even if it means leaving a message on an automatic recording system.

School governors

The governing body ensures that the school delivers a good quality education for all pupils. They have a strategic role, working closely with the head teacher to set the school's aims and policies. In so doing, they monitor the school's standards, holding the head to account for that performance, overseeing finance management and making sure money is properly spent.

Pupil well-being is part of their remit, including behaviour and discipline, safety, promoting community cohesion and safeguarding. They are involved in hearing appeals and grievances, including admission appeals and exclusions, and in setting the school behaviour policy. Members will be allocated responsibility for looked after children and safeguarding.

Governors are volunteers committed to supporting the school, pupils and staff, and to improving the school as much as possible. They draw on a variety of backgrounds and skills, and typically include parents and representatives from the local community alongside the head and other teachers.

Head teacher

The head, sometimes called the principal, is the most senior person in the organisation and has overall responsibility for every aspect of school life.

In smaller schools, you may have more day-to-day contact with them; for instance, they will take a role in problem-solving, special education and/or meeting the needs of looked after children. In larger or inner-city schools, these functions will be delegated to staff – for example, the year head or head of department – who carry out their responsibilities on behalf of the school and the head teacher.

Head of year

The head of year has responsibility for the year group. They will have in place a system to monitor children and young people's progress and to ensure that they are able to reach their potential by removing barriers to achievement. Therefore, they should be aware of and take into account pupils' academic, social and relationship issues, and lead on actions to address these.

Their role is broad, with the overall goal of promoting achievement and well-being. This aspect is sometimes called "pastoral care".

Head of department

The head of department takes responsibility for their subject – the curriculum and how it is taught.

As with everyone in the school, they have a role in promoting achievement. They can be useful to contact if, for example, a child or young person has a problem with a particular subject or needs some extra help.

Pastoral support

Pastoral support concerns ways of promoting pupils' well-being and varies according to different schools. One approach is for the school to employ a learning mentor who helps pupils to deal with any individual difficulties or issues that might affect their learning. Mentors may help with issues such as poor attendance, low self-esteem and confidence, behaviour or emotional difficulties, settling into a school, bereavement or problems at home. They may work with a pupil on a one-to-one basis or run small groups around a particular area, such as anger management.

Some schools also run nurture groups. Led by teachers in school, these seek to replace missing or distorted early nurturing experiences for both children and young adults by immersing them in an accepting and warm environment. They offer the opportunity to experience the early nurturing experiences some children and young people lack – especially those looked after – giving them the skills to do well at school, make friends and deal more confidently with life.

Special educational needs co-ordinators (SENCOs)

All schools must appoint a qualified, experienced teacher as the special needs co-ordinator, universally known as the SENCO. She or he takes responsibility for children and young people with special needs, with or without an EHC plan (see Chapter 9) and makes sure that the school implements their special educational needs (SEN) policy.

A key element of their role is working in partnership with their colleagues to co-ordinate the additional support children and young people need in order to achieve their potential. They also work closely with a wide range of other professionals such as educational psychologists and speech and language therapists.

In a small school, the SENCO role may be fulfilled by a senior teacher with other responsibilities, such as the deputy head. Larger schools may have a SEN team with more than one SENCO.

Communication with the SENCO is a two-way process. They are a valuable source of information about the progress of each child or young person. Also, they can feed relevant information about the child at home into the school's approach and strategies. They should attend PEP and other meetings regarding a child or young person with special educational needs and contribute to decision-making.

The SENCO is therefore an important point of contact for foster carers looking after children and young people with special educational needs. They are a source of guidance and advice themselves, can intercede on the child's behalf with other teachers, and assist the process of assessing the nature and level of each individual child's needs. (You will find more on SEN provision in Chapter 9.)

Education welfare officers

Education welfare officers work with schools, pupils, parents and carers to support regular attendance. They become involved with families when a child is failing to attend school at an expected level or is regularly late. Children are legally required to go to school and the education welfare officer is empowered to take action through a court if a child consistently fails to attend. They are also there to support families and identify difficulties that need attention. They will support relationship building between schools and families and will attend meetings in the school and family home.

Key points

- If you want to get things done for the child or young person in your care, the VSH is your ally. They are experts in their field and carry considerable weight in their education authority. They can influence decisions about the child's educational needs and the allocation of resources to meet them.
- It is important to understand how schools function and who's who. School secretaries are the hub and heart of schools, especially at primary level. They know what's going on. They have personal contact, they arrange the head teacher's diary, book rooms and through this they have an insight into the school organisation. Get to know them.
- Working alongside the SENCO is essential if your child or young person has special educational needs. They are "in-school experts". They can work with their teaching colleagues to make sure your child's needs are understood and met and can recommend extra learning resources as part of the PEP. If your child changes school, for instance from primary to secondary, they can provide vital continuity, reaching out to their counterparts in the new school and being part of the transfer planning process.
- Make yourself familiar with these different roles. No policy, procedure or practice guide is a substitute for a working relationship. Get to know the people you are likely to have most contact with, such as the designated teacher and the SENCO if your child has special needs. It shows them the child is cared for and cared about, and that what happens in school is supported by you in the home. They can get things done for children. They are problem-solvers, and perhaps more importantly, they can be proactive in making sure problems don't occur in the first place.

5 Choosing a school: primary and secondary

Education is about enabling children and young people to achieve their full potential, to be the best they can be. It's about watching them grow into adulthood, having friends and interests and the same opportunities as their peers.

Although social workers tend to be responsible for choosing and securing a school place, foster carers have an important role to play. In a recent study of looked after children and education by TACT (a fostering and adoption provider) (2018) almost a third (30 per cent) of foster carers surveyed said they hadn't been involved in this choice. This is not how it should be. It is essential that you not only participate in this decision but also listen to the concerns of your child. (The same study found that 43 per cent of the children interviewed said they were given no say in where they went to school.)

Choosing a school is an example of what being child centred means in practice. Foster carers are experts in the children they care for. This knowledge about who they are, their unique individuality and their needs is central when it comes to finding the right school. Also, you have to play your part in making it work. You visit the school, attend open days, meet teachers and pupils, absorb information, make sure homework is done and judge the school's performance.

Decision-making

The local authority is at the centre of decision-making about which school or college a child or young person attends, as it is for any significant decision regarding a looked after child. Here it is worth knowing that the Government's statutory admissions code states that schools must give pupils in local authority care the "highest priority" (Department for Education, 2014b, para 1.7).

Arrangements for choosing a school are contained in the child or young person's Placement Plan. Education is a major element of the child care planning process, i.e. part of their Care Plan discussed at reviews and in PEPs (see Chapter 3). Good practice is for the foster carer and social worker to share this responsibility. The VSH must also be involved.

If the child or young person is subject to a care order, the local authority takes the decision. Parents will be consulted, depending on the nature and extent of their involvement with the child or young person. If they are accommodated under section 20, the parent (i.e. those with parental responsibility) must be fully involved and take part in decision-making.

Making the choice

As far as you can, choose the primary or secondary school that best meets your child's needs (see Appendix for details of the different types of school available). You will have high aspirations for her, so look for somewhere that will encourage her without being unduly competitive, but at the same time balance this with not wanting to push her beyond her capabilities.

Think about the nature and level of any help she might need. Match this to the pastoral care and extra support each school offers. Take the social side into account too – extra-curricular activities, where her friends are going.

The journey to and from school is another factor. Can she manage a lengthy journey? Does the route have any serious risk factors? This relates to the young person's self-awareness and ability to protect herself when out in public.

Weigh up all the factors, just as we would for our own children (see Box below for where to go for information).

Sources of information

- Ofsted inspection reports: these are public documents available at https://reports.ofsted.gov.uk/. All schools receive a rating, e.g. "poor", "good", "outstanding". Schools with an inadequate rating must be avoided. But dig deeper than the overall assessment. The reports list what the school does well, and not so well, including academic achievement, the range of subjects offered, how safe the school is, its ethos. Compare this to the needs of the child or young person.
- The school's website: here the aims of the school and its ethos are set out.
- A school visit: visit local schools and take the child in your care along so that she feels part of the process.
- Local knowledge: communities hold a wealth of knowledge about what schools are like. Take a balanced view, but take this knowledge seriously. If possible, talk to parents with children at the school and talk to those children or young people.
- Look on internet forums such as www.mumsnet.com.
- Get to know your local school: over time, it helps to get to know the ones in your catchment area, especially at primary level. Partly this is about understanding what they can offer a child in your care; partly it is about them knowing you. Schools feel reassured if they know carers and that the child's social worker will support them.

Admissions policies and criteria

It is compulsory for all children to start school at the beginning of the term after their fifth birthday. Your local authority is obliged to offer every child a place.

As stated earlier, looked after children must be given the highest priority. This applies even if the school is oversubscribed and care must be taken to prevent head teachers avoiding admissions or making the process difficult. If this is the case, those seeking to secure a place for their child should contact the person in the local authority responsible for school admissions.

Admission criteria

Each individual school or local authority sets its own admission criteria. These are different for each school and may include children:

- having a sibling at the school already;
- living close to the school;
- following a particular religion (for faith schools);
- doing well in an entrance exam (for selective schools such as grammar or stage schools);
- going to a particular primary school (a "feeder" school);
- being eligible for the pupil premium.

Because they have the highest priority, regardless of these criteria, looked after children effectively have first choice.

It is not possible to choose a school where a child or young person has already been excluded. However, applications must be accepted even if the school is oversubscribed and/or class sizes have reached a maximum. Faith schools are an exception. They will prioritise looked after children of that faith over those from other religions.

Where the school chosen is an academy, the situation is more blurred. These are publicly funded independent schools. The local authority can ask the school to admit a child or young person but cannot compel them. The guidance states that usually an agreement can be reached. If not, the authority can ask the Secretary of State to intervene. This appeal goes to adjudication, one outcome being that the academy is directed to take the child. While there is a sense from the official guidance that agreement should be reached in most cases, this does potentially disadvantage looked after children.

All local authority websites should provide links to advice and guidance on how to apply for a school place and how to contact those responsible for the admission process.

A huge disadvantage for looked after children can be the time taken to establish a place and transfer to a new school. Therefore, local authorities set a maximum time limit of 20 school days within which they must secure an education placement for any looked after child. This means a full-time place in a local mainstream school unless the needs of the child make full-time or local or mainstream provision unsuitable (see www.gov.uk/schools-admissions/admissions-criteria).

Some independent and grammar schools may select individual pupils based on ability or talent in a specialist area: for example, science, maths, sport, drama or languages. In this case, you will need to consult with the individual school and their application process approximately a year before your child is due to start. Entrance under these criteria may include exams and interviews.

Choosing a primary school

Children in England generally start school in the September after their fourth birthday. However, a child reaches compulsory school age on the "prescribed day" following his fifth birthday. The prescribed days are 31 December, 31 March and 31 August.

Here are a few key questions to consider when helping to choose your child's primary school. They are adapted from a selection of points listed by the adoption agency PAC-UK and are equally relevant for foster carers. Above all 'look for flexible schools that are willing to listen and learn and are proactive about developing support to meet each child's needs'.

How does the school provide consistent key relationships for children with attachment needs?

For example:

- named members of staff as key workers for children, with quality 1:1 time scheduled into the child's day or week, with particular attention to the times when the child is most vulnerable;
- staff who are aware of how to let the child know that they are held in mind;
- ways to help children stay connected, e.g. a postcard in the holidays?

Where is the safe base for children when they need to calm down or regulate?

- Is there a nurture group and how do they prioritise children to be part of this?
- Is it used as a planned daily intervention?

- Is there a nurture space or calming zone that children can access as and when needed with a key member of staff?

What is the behaviour management policy?

For example:

- Does the school apply the policy flexibly to best meet the needs of each child, e.g. if they use a yellow/red card system or a "sunshine–storm clouds" system for moving children "up" and "down" based on their behaviour, will they use a different non-shaming strategy for your child?
- Does the school see behaviour as communication and focus on meeting those needs?
- What is the school's approach to exclusion?

What support is in place for children who find unstructured times difficult?

For example:

- Is there an indoor lunch club for more vulnerable children, where they can develop their social skills, or calm down and relax?
- Do the midday supervisors organise structured games in the playground?
- Are there systems for children who want to play with friends, e.g. a buddy system or a friendship bench?

How does the school provide structure and consistency?

For example:

- sticking to the timetable at Christmas and ends of terms;
- letting parents/carers and children know as soon as possible about staff changes and supply teachers;
- providing a schedule for parents/carers to prepare the child at home;
- using visual timetables to let children know about upcoming changes.

How does the school share the information you give them about the child's background and needs?

For example:

- internal information sharing systems;
- meetings, policies...
- If this is on a "need to know" basis, how is this decided and clarified with everyone including parents/carers?

How does the school share information with parents/carers?

For example:

- Does the class teacher speak to parents/carers at the end of the day, or call home?
- Are staff able to email parents/carers if needed?
- Is there a text message system, e.g. to notify parents/carers about snow days?

How has the school used its Pupil Premium Plus for looked after pupils?

For example:

- Is it used for social and emotional interventions or only learning?
- Is the Pupil Premium Plus clearly differentiated from the overall pupil premium pot for children entitled to free school meals?

How does the school manage curriculum hotspots, i.e. issues that might trigger your child?

For example:

- Does it liaise with parents/carers about baby photos and family trees?
- Does it approach with sensitivity cards for mother's and father's day; subjects such as evacuees in WW2 in English and History; NSPCC and Children in Need assemblies?

Choosing a secondary school

Many of the questions you would need to ask overlap with those already discussed. That said, several additional points relating to secondary education need to be considered when you are visiting schools to make your decision.

If your child is transferring from primary to secondary education, narrow down the choice using your own research, then visit together. Ask to talk to any of the school staff who might have a particular role to play in your child's education. On public visiting days, schools naturally emphasise their facilities and academic achievements, all of which are important, but you may want to talk to teaching staff with responsibility for pastoral care and/or the designated teacher, perhaps the SENCO.

These questions, too, are adapted from information compiled by PAC-UK and reproduced in our companion handbook for adopters (Fursland, 2018, pp. 102–105).

How does the school provide consistent key relationships for children with attachment needs?

For example:

- vertical form tutors;
- nurture time/group;
- non-teaching pastoral staff available throughout day;
- learning mentors;
- for children who receive one-to-one support, is support organised by child (i.e. one consistent teaching assistant) or by subject (i.e. up to 10 teaching assistants)?

Where is the safe base for children when they need to calm down or regulate?

For example:

- How does this work? Drop-in basis?
- Does the child need specific permission to attend?
- How is it staffed and supervised?

What is the behaviour management policy?

For example:

- Does the school recognise that cause-and-effect consequences may not be effective for children with histories of trauma and loss?

- Does the school apply the policy flexibly to best meet the needs of each child?
- How does the school moderate its use of detention or isolation for children who may be re-traumatised by these approaches?

What support is in place for children who find unstructured times difficult?

For example:

- lunch club;
- drop-in base;
- structured games on playground;
- social skills groups...are any drop-in spaces staffed consistently?

How does the school provide structure and consistency?

For example:

- Year 7 in permanent base;
- lockers for children's belongings;
- vertical form tutor;
- approach to staff sickness and supply teachers;
- advance warning of timetable changes, building work, etc.;
- timetable on website so parents/carers can prepare child at home.

How does the school support the Year 6 to Year 7 transition?

For example:

- extra visits for vulnerable children;
- opportunities to see the school both empty and busy;
- maps and photographs;
- summer club to get used to the school and key staff?

How does the school share information with parents/carers?

For example:

- what equipment/kit is needed;
- homework timetable;
- Is there a web-based supported learning environment? Is this used by all staff? Do parents have log-ins?

How does the school support children who find it difficult to manage their feelings?

For example:

- nurture group;
- calm boxes;
- a calming zone within the school;
- emotion regulation skills teaching and coaching;
- anger management coaching;
- empathy from all staff.

How does the school manage curriculum hotspots, i.e. issues which might trigger your child?

For example:

- liaise with parents about sex, alcohol, drugs education;
- pass on information about any particular triggers to members of teaching staff.

Key points

- When it comes to choosing a school for the child in your care, the local authority is at the centre of decision-making; arrangements are contained in the child's Placement Plan.
- Research the schools in your area – look at their websites, talk to local parents and visit schools with the child in your care.

- When it comes to choosing a primary school, as far as you can, look for a supportive, nurturing environment, a flexible behaviour management policy, and good structure and consistency.
- Secondary schools, too, need to provide a safe base and support such as learning mentors, good communication systems and awareness of issues that might trigger your child.
- Remember that looked after children must be given the highest priority, even if the school is oversubscribed.

6 Supporting your child in school

What your child will learn obviously depends on his age and stage of development. In England, the National Curriculum – with its 12 core subjects listed below – provides the framework for what is taught in most schools, from primary school reception classes through to colleges of further education. But there is far more to school than learning academic subjects: sports, after-school clubs, music, outings and gaining social skills through daily interactions with others are all important parts of school life. At the same time, navigating all these experiences is seldom easy, especially for looked after children, and depending on their circumstances your child will need a lot of support. For example, those fostering lone asylum-seeking and refugee young people will know that a primary need will be language support (see Chapter 7).

What is the National Curriculum?

The majority of schools teach the National Curriculum. It is not compulsory for independent schools or academies to do so but most do.

The National Curriculum comprises a set of subjects outlining what pupils should be taught and the standards they should reach in each subject. The subjects taught at **primary school** (Key Stages 1 and 2) are:

- English
- maths
- science
- design and technology
- history
- geography
- art and design
- music

- physical education (PE), including swimming
- computing
- foreign languages (at Key Stage 2)

Schools must also provide religious education (RE) and sex education – although parents/carers and guardians can ask for their children to be taken out of the whole lesson or part of it. Schools often also teach personal, social and health education (PSHE) and citizenship.

In **secondary school**, in Key Stage 3, pupils will study the above subjects but probably in more detail: for example, within design and technology they may specifically be taught textiles, food technology and resistant materials. Pupils are then able to select their options for Key Stage 4, but this will include English, maths and science. Some schools also make other subjects compulsory such as computing or a modern foreign language. This is something you will need to check with the individual school. Subjects for those beyond 16 years of age are more diverse: young people have the opportunity to study for academic qualifications in the form of A-levels or diplomas and work-based training in the form of apprenticeships. New A-level subjects are regularly introduced and may include areas such as dance and drama, criminology, electronics, film studies and world development.

Apprenticeships are available for young people aged 16 and over, and incorporate a combination of training onsite, attendance at college and work experience. This then leads to a qualification as well as receiving a wage. Many areas of work offer apprenticeships, such as businesses engaged in technical, manual, administrative and creative work or the services industry (see www.gov.uk/apprenticeships-guide). (For more on post-16 education see Chapter 10.)

Are there other options?

Some schools (such as private schools or academies) do not have to teach the National Curriculum and may choose to follow another programme, such as the Cambridge Primary or International Primary Curriculums (see www.cambridgeinternational.org/programmes-and-qualifications/cambridge-primary/curriculum/ and www.greatlearning.com/ipc/). Schools work with these schemes to deliver the teaching that they feel best suits their children.

Whatever curriculum it is following, each school needs to demonstrate children's learning and progress. Private schools are inspected by the Independent Schools Inspectorate (ISI) and academies are subject to inspection by Ofsted.

How will my child be taught?

Teaching methods have changed over the years and some of us were taught quite differently in subjects such as reading and maths. It can be daunting when a child asks for help or if you sit and read with a child, or offer to help with maths homework only to find that the type of work being set is totally unfamiliar! First of all, don't worry – enjoy learning together. You don't have to be an expert. It's your attitude that matters together with your willingness to dedicate time and attention to the child or young person in your care. Children need to see that learning can be hard but that there are ways of overcoming difficulties.

Reading is particularly important here (see Chapter 7).

Checking progress

How will my child be assessed?

Children are assessed in many different ways: set tasks, projects, verbal discussion, homework, tests and exams. These fit into two types of assessment: day-to-day feedback and progress checks.

Day-to-day feedback refers to ongoing information that feeds into the learning process. This might include verbal feedback from a teacher, written feedback on work and targets being set.

Progress checks usually consist of a test or exam given at the end of a set piece of work, such as at the end of a half-term or school year. This includes SATs tests, GCSEs and A-levels. They also include "teacher assessments", perhaps where a teacher rather than someone from outside the school is observing a child with a task or marking his work. The aim is to assess the broad level a child has reached at a given time.

What should I expect my child to be tested on and when?

- In Key Stage 1 (Year 1), a phonics screening test is carried out. This is where a child's ability to "decode" words for reading is assessed.
- At the end of Key Stage 1 (Year 2), national tests (SATs) and teacher assessments are carried out in English, maths and science.
- At the end of Key Stage 2 (Year 6), national tests (SATs) and teacher assessments are carried out in English and maths, and teacher assessments in science. Children aiming for a place at one of England's 164 grammar schools take the 11-plus.
- At the end of Key Stage 4 (Year 11), GCSEs take place.
- In addition, pupils are often tested throughout the year and at the end of each school year by the school.

Age	Year group	Stage	Tests	Considerations
3–4		Pre-school		Apply for primary school place
4–5	Reception	Foundation	Early Years Foundation Stage Profile	
5–6 6–7	Year 1 Year 2	Key Stage 1	National tests and tasks in numeracy and literacy (SATS)	
7–8 8–9 9–10 10–11	Year 3 Year 4 Year 5 Year 6	Key Stage 2	National tests and tasks in numeracy and literacy SATS/11-plus	Apply for a secondary school place

11–12 12–13 13–14	Year 7 Year 8 Year 9	Key Stage 3	School internal tests	Choose options for Years 10 and 11
14–15 15-16	Year 10 Year 11	Key Stage 4	GCSEs or other vocational qualifications	Apply for sixth form, college or apprenticeship
16–17 17–18	Year 12 Year 13 (if at sixth form)		A levels Post-16 qualifications Apprenticeships	HE options and careers service
18 +			Undergraduate certificates, diplomas, degrees, HNC, HND, work based qualifications	Careers service

How far are children expected to achieve?

GCSEs

Expectations are that pupils will achieve five GCSEs level 4 or above (previously grades A*–C) including English and maths. The assessment of English and maths has recently been changed to a numerical system from 9 to 1 (9 being the highest grade). Pupils will be expected to gain a level 4 or above in order to re-sit the exam; levels 1–3 are considered a fail. Looked after children significantly underperform compared to their peers, but continually stress how they wish that their carers, teachers and professionals had demanded higher expectations from them. Like 12-year-old Amy, quoted below, whose foster carer supported her to take her 11-plus, those who do well in education tend to say that they had support and encouragement at home:

Sue, my foster carer, explained to me from the very beginning how important getting an education was and how it could give me choices and change my life for the better when I grow up. In Year 6, she encouraged me to enter for the 11-plus as she believed I was capable though my teacher disagreed. My social worker Andrea also supported me all the way. Having only 10 weeks to prepare for the exam, Sue provided me with a tutor and I had some lessons on the weekend using workbooks with Sue.

I was really pleased with myself for getting into grammar school, but mostly I am proud of getting my mum and nan being proud of me. I can't remember one time I made them proud, and I found out that I had passed my 11-plus the day I saw my nan, which made it more special.

A-levels and other options

In Years 10 and 11, pupils will need to consider their next steps in education. This will depend on their future career paths, their academic achievement and, importantly, their likes and abilities. The school will have a career guidance adviser and it is important for your child to meet with them to discuss options. Supporting young adults at this stage is vital for their own engagement in education, so exploration of FE and HE colleges and apprenticeship schemes, in addition to A-level options, is essential (see Chapter 10 on post-16 education).

Attending special evenings

It is important to attend parents'/carers' evenings and open evenings to become familiar with the school and teachers. Nowadays discussions between teachers and parents/carers are usually informal and co-operative. As the following case study shows, there is no longer any need for anyone to become anxious when receiving information from the school or to dread meeting a teacher – despite the foster carer's anxiety, the discussions dwelt on the child's best interest and led to a positive outcome.

Lena

Lena [a foster carer] had received details from Bradley's school about a parent/carer evening that was coming up. Bradley was in Year 6. Lena was not too worried about attending as she had spoken to Bradley's teacher at the school door at collection time earlier in the year, and thought things were going fairly well, even if Bradley was a little behind academically. She couldn't remember her own parents' evenings at school, other than that they gave her a feeling of dread, so she was happy to avoid them and had decided not to go.

Bradley's teacher called Lena and encouraged her to book an appointment and attend with Bradley, as this was a time for sharing work and discussing things that they had been learning in class. Although reluctant to attend, Lena arranged the appointment and headed to the parents' evening with Bradley. She was surprised by how things had changed since she had attended school. She went into Bradley's classroom where he was keen to show her his work displayed on the wall. It was a piece of work on describing a setting in literacy. He had worked particularly hard on this and was proud that it was on display. Lena sat with his teacher and, together with Bradley, looked through his work and spotted areas where he was very good and those that needed further attention. The teacher identified things that Bradley could work on at home and Lena felt encouraged that she could support him with this.

Later that evening, she commented:

'It was so much more enjoyable than I had thought it would be! It was great to look at Bradley's work and to see him so enthusiastic. Normally when I ask him what he has been doing at school he says, "Nothing much".'

As the teacher explained:

'It is really important for parents/carers to attend. It is much more about having the opportunity to share work and see what is going well as well as what the next steps are. We work in a triad – the school [me the teacher], the child and the parent/carer. We need to work together to support progress and that starts with talking about it.'

Children are taught within different teaching groups at school. Often in primary schools this is done in mixed ability groups. In some subjects such as English and maths, children may be put into ability sets, in which those of higher, middle and lower abilities sit and work together. This means that the tasks they are set and the support they receive in class meet their needs at the level at which they are currently working. Groups may change throughout the year depending on the topic area being taught and your child's and other children's progress within the group.

In secondary schools a system called "banding" is often used. This is where pupils are grouped broadly depending on their ability and then taught within these groups for most subjects like history, geography and science; sometimes English and maths are more specifically set.

Attachment figures and having a "key person" in school

Building trust and attachment can be difficult for class teachers when they do not have much time with the child every day and they have limited time to give one-to-one attention. Nonetheless, it is important for a child to have the opportunity to build attachment with one or two "safe" adults in school – which may be the teacher, a learning assistant, key worker or someone else who acts as a mentor and attachment figure.

Some schools identify a key member of staff for a child who has difficulties regulating his emotions, such as a mentor or teaching assistant. The designated teacher also has a role to play here.

The school identifies a person in school who is well placed to regulate that child and how they will do it. This should be done in consultation with the child or young person and the carer. That person is sent for if the child is, for instance, having an angry outburst or a panic attack in the classroom. The key person will ideally get to know and understand the child well, build trust, anticipate his needs and difficulties and advocate for him within the school. In time, they may be able to help the child develop his reflective skills, emotional literacy and social skills.

Children could see their key person every morning when they arrive at school, or at break-time or the end of the school day, so they can discuss anything that is making them worried, upset or angry. The key person is someone who will provide one-to-one attention, listen and care when things are not going well, celebrate when things do go well and acknowledge the challenges for the child. They may, for example, play turn-taking or trust games, or there might be a "bucket" where the child can put in people or things he doesn't like or is worried about.

Here's an example:

> *Seven-year-old Dante regularly had outbursts in both the classroom and at lunchtime. Through a process of really getting alongside Dante...and together with the support of attachment-informed consultation sessions, his teaching assistant was able to find several strategies that were effective in reducing incidents and increasing positive moments. Some of these included: having a personalised sensory box; starting the morning with drumming sessions; having a zen zone filled with items such as weighted blankets and bubbles; using picture checklists; and having outdoor brain breaks.*
>
> (Treisman, 2017, p. 156)

Recognising behaviour as "communication"

Biting, hitting, kicking, shouting, swearing, running out of the classroom... For a teacher attempting to teach a class of 30 children, a child or young person who disrupts lessons in this way can make teaching pretty much impossible, especially when the usual methods do not prove effective – or even prove counterproductive.

A different approach is needed, which starts with understanding why he behaves as he does.

Teachers need to know how to manage such behaviour – for the sake of the child, for the sake of the other children in the class, and for their own sake, because having to deal with it every working day can be incredibly stressful. As Nicola Marshall writes in relation to attachment and special needs education:

> *Probably the hardest and most important area for schools to address is our obsession with modifying behaviour. What we have at the moment are systems that essentially work on the premise that children and young people have the same level of respect for authority that they used to have and, indeed, that they all have the same understanding as each other and the ability to change their behaviour when we tell them to.*
>
> *Zone boards, sticker charts, marble jars, sun and dark clouds, house points, incentive schemes, yellow and red cards, isolations, detentions, time outs and exclusions all rely on a child's ability to join the dots between their behaviour and the consequences. If I know that when I speed in my car I*

> *might kill someone and end up in prison, does it stop me speeding? It should, and most of the time it does, but there are odd occasions when I forget, or maybe my anxiety over being late, or whatever it might be, takes over and drives my behaviour to ignore the rules.*
>
> *Children and young people who've not had the chance to develop cause and effect thinking and may be operating in the survival part of their brain cannot manage their behaviour just because we move them down the zone board or show them a red card. In fact, for some children, being "on a red" gets them the most attention and that's what they most crave. They need someone to notice that they are struggling and to keep them safe.*
>
> *Moving away from these punitive, shame-riddled systems will take time and can be messy. We have to concentrate on relationships and understanding the child's experience of school. We may even have to change our approach to certain children, when we consider what their early experiences might have been like.*
>
> (Marshall, 2018)

Successfully managing behaviour in children and young people with emotional, social and behavioural difficulties requires teachers, other school staff and carers to understand something about the impact of trauma on the brain, to see behaviour as "communication", and to develop strategies for successful intervention that are based on the importance of attachment, warm and empathic relationships, and increasing the child or young person's feelings of safety and decreasing his feelings of anxiety.

As a foster carer, you are in a position to help teachers to "get" your child. By working with the school you can bring about change.

Sensory issues

Schools and teachers need to be ready to make adjustments for children with sensory issues. For example:

- The school or classroom can set up a "safe corner", a calm area or cosy nurture room to which the child can withdraw when feeling overwhelmed. Some schools already have such special spaces for pupils with autism.

- Children who are bothered by noise may find it helpful to wear noise-blocking headphones.
- Some children may need to sit somewhere away from the lights or windows if they find it too bright.
- Those who find the feel of certain items of the school uniform unpleasant might need permission to wear something different.
- Other adjustments might include the child being able to do tasks that help him to avoid the playground at break time, if that is overwhelming, or allowing him to eat his lunch somewhere other than the school dining hall.

Encouraging friendships

More and more schools are addressing children and young people's social difficulties and recognising the need to promote kind and caring behaviour, to encourage children's friendships and tackle bullying. The rise of cyber bullying – any form of bullying that takes place online or through smartphones and tablets – has made this task more complicated (see Chapters 8 and 9 for more on the internet and bullying).

Methods that schools are using include:

- nurture groups;
- a buddy system, where the teacher puts into place special friends or friendship groups for children who are new to the school or who are struggling to make friends;
- peer mentors – often children from higher years in the school who can work with younger ones to encourage friendships or to give them someone to talk to if they are worried or upset;
- playground games organised by trained lunchtime supervisors to help children make friends, to provide structure at playtime and to reduce conflict in the playground;
- lunchtime and after-school clubs for Lego, ICT, Pokemon, etc. so that vulnerable students have genuine options for somewhere to go if they don't like the playground or the football field, or if they find it easier to interact with other children over a structured activity.

Celebrating success

Some children and young people are very fearful of making mistakes because they have learned in their early life that doing something wrong will incur an adult's anger or punishment. Fear of making mistakes can lead to them being unable to take part in classroom activities; they are too anxious that they will fail.

Finding something they are good at can really help. If they do not excel in the classroom, they may enjoy music or school sports, or joining a choir or out-of-school activity or club such as swimming, Brownies or Scouts, or keeping chickens. Anything out of school that helps build their self-esteem will have a positive knock-on effect in school too.

Some children and young people find praise hard to take, so it needs to be chosen and delivered with care. If a child cannot accept praise or sabotages attempts to reward him, you (and the teacher) need to find other ways to do it – for example, praise what he has done rather than praising the child himself: 'That little girl was so pleased when you shared with her' rather than 'You are a good boy.' Praising in private might be easier rather than in front of everyone, and praising in non-verbal ways with a high-five or pat on the back can work well. Being specific is also good: 'I like the way you have used those bright colours in your picture' rather than simply: 'That's lovely.'

Further issues

Recognising trauma triggers and sensitive issues in the curriculum

If teachers know about these triggers they can help your child avoid them in the classroom. Make the teacher and school aware (though not necessarily give all the details) so that they can make some adjustments, for example, around Mother's Day or family tree activities, as well as drug awareness and sexual health lessons.

Recognising that a child may be functioning as a much younger child

As we saw in our opening chapter, children and young people who have missed out on early nurturing experiences may be delayed in their emotional development and have the needs and behaviour of a much younger child. So it is helpful for the teacher to adjust expectations and use approaches targeted to the child's emotional age rather than his actual chronological age.

Helping a child with executive functioning difficulties

For a child or young person who struggles to organise themselves, remember things, follow instructions and manage tasks, these strategies can help:

- Having a mentor/one-to-one time with a member of the school staff at the start and the end of the school day, or with whom they can "check in" at certain points to make sure they have everything they need, have understood homework tasks, know where to go next, and so on.
- When giving instructions, the teacher can use the child or young person's name first, to get attention, then give precise, rather than general instructions. For example: 'Kevin, go to the changing room and put on your gym kit and trainers' rather than just 'Get ready for gym.'
- Tasks should be broken down into manageable chunks to help the child or young person understand how to tackle them.
- The school can keep spare gym kits, pencil cases and so on for children who have forgotten to bring theirs.
- Visual timetables at home and school, which show the child or young person in pictures and with simple words what he needs to do when (e.g. getting ready for school) or what exactly will be the sequence of events on that day in school. The pictures on the visual timetable can be photographs of the child or young person doing the various activities, which will help him relate to it.
- Together with your child, get school clothes and a school bag ready every evening so that it is organised in the morning with no last-minute panics. Get into a routine of packing the bag and checking off a list all the things he needs to take each day (consulting the visual timetable).

- Help your child with time management of homework, prioritising urgent tasks but ensuring that he doesn't forget the less urgent tasks.
- At secondary school, you may need to sign a planner for the start of the week – try to remember to do this on Sunday evenings.

Key points

- Familiarise yourself with the National Curriculum and how your child will be taught and assessed. The more you know and understand how it all works the better you will be able to support him.
- Be sure to attend parents'/carers' evenings. Remember that teachers and other staff will have your child's best interests in mind.
- Professionals in the fields of trauma, attachment and FASD, academics and support organisations such as Fostering Network are working hard to get the message through to schools and teachers across the country so that they can make the adjustments children need and support them to achieve all they are capable of.
- The more that you, as a foster carer, know and understand about your child's needs and behaviour, and the techniques that work for him, the more you will be able to help guide the school.
- Encourage friendships; as more schools acknowledge children's social difficulties and the rise of issues such as cyber bullying, methods to tackle these should be in place. If you feel these are lacking, request that the school provides support in the form of nurture groups, peer mentors or a buddy system.

7 Supporting children's and young people's learning at home

Carer (or parental) involvement in children's learning has a dynamic effect on progress. Many researchers believe that the home presents the most powerful teaching and learning situation. When caregivers show interest in their children's experiences and activities, children's motivation and self-esteem grows.

(Pallett, Simmonds and Warman, 2010, p. 29)

School and family life are closely linked. As we emphasise throughout this book, support from foster carers can have a significant impact on children's attitudes to learning, their aspirations and confidence to make the most of any opportunities open to them. As Clare Pallett and colleagues (2010) point out in their foster carer training programme for supporting children's learning, 'Schools may frustrate this or they may enhance it.' Whatever the case, it is important that you keep in mind that education is an important aspect of care and try to keep abreast of what is going on in terms of your child's engagement with learning and subsequent attainment as well as her overall well-being. Central to this is the acquisition of reading skills. To quote again from Pallett and others (2010, p. iv): 'It is very difficult to learn without being able to read; it is also very difficult to become independent without being able to read.'

The importance of reading

Reading is important not only for developing children's literacy skills and helping educational achievement but also for bonding with your child, building a relationship of trust and security that comes from her knowing that you have chosen to spend time with her and she has your undivided attention. The benefits of "quality time" spent reading together can be far reaching. In addition to helping your child learn to "look" and build her vocabulary, it tells her that she is your priority.

A survey into reading and foster carers, commissioned by the Book Trust (2017), found that the more frequently a carer read with their foster child, the greater the positive influence on their relationship.

These two foster carers highlight the benefits of reading with the children in their care:

> *... to build a relationship, to build trust, to show them that people do want to spend time with them... and to build their self-worth, I guess that you know, people do want to help them and be interested in what they want to be interested in.*
>
> *... it signified the end of the day and did not matter if there was upset or behaviour issues... we could still do it... and it was nice to do that at the end of the day to show that we still cared about them, no matter what had happened that day.*
>
> (Rix, Lea and Edwards, 2017, p. 10)

The all-round benefits of reading are reiterated in many of the survey's findings:

- Around three-quarters of carers strongly agreed that reading helped to widen a child's vocabulary, to feed imagination, to help with schoolwork and build communication skills.
- Foster children often made reference to the importance of reading for their schoolwork and learning. For example: 'I think it's really important to read because you can learn more.'
- Over two-thirds of children reported that reading made them feel happy.
- Foster carers, too, highlighted the positive impacts of reading on children's mood and behaviour. They commented on the foster child having increased confidence and self-esteem and that reading had a calming effect: 'It does seem to calm them...it's just a lovely togetherness end to the day.'
- Many of the children interviewed said their views of reading had changed since being in the placement. This was generally attributed to the foster carer making reading fun and enjoyable. Carers also described how important it was to find the right book to inspire children to read. Once

a child was inspired, it generally became much easier to sustain that motivation and delight in reading.

- Less than half of the foster carers had received support with helping their foster child to read. Of those who had, two-thirds had received it from the child's school and half from the local authority. The support provided by friends and family, libraries, schools and local authorities was the most useful. However, for some foster carers the child's school was a barrier to encouraging children to read. For instance, some reported schools sending children home with books below the child's level. In others, participation in reading schemes at school had led to damaged self-esteem for children.

The full report from the Book Trust research, *Reading in Foster Families* by Katie Rix, Jo Lea and Amy Edwards, is freely available at www.booktrust.org.uk/globalassets/resources/research/reading-in-foster-families-full-report.pdf.

Here are a few specific tips:

- Put aside a regular time, say 20 minutes a day, five days a week to read with your child, teenagers included. When VSH Fiona Lewis persuaded a group of foster carers to do this for 10 weeks the results were remarkable: the young people's average reading ages went up from nine years to 13 years and nine months!

  One child, Jason, who has ADHD and has never enjoyed reading before, actually improved his reading age by five years and three months, and his carer, Sue, now reports that he is reading voraciously, and independently. He also selected some cookery books as part of his choices (children were able to select from a warehouse of titles and once completed, could keep the books and choose more) so was experimenting with baking as well.

  (www.thefosteringnetwork.org.uk/blogs/foster-care-fortnight/importance-reading-view-virtual-school-head)

- Remember that reading is not just about words. It's about communication between child and carer and learning to look.
- At the earlier end of the age range (five to seven years) in Key Stage 1, children often bring a book home. Try to read this with them every night. If your child finds it difficult, try one page each or get her to describe what is happening in the pictures.

- Reading for pleasure is important. If your child finds reading stressful and difficult, focus on discussing the story rather than "decoding" the words.
- Reading doesn't have to stop when you put the book down. Talk to your child about books you've read and books you think she might enjoy. Point out connections between everyday events and stories you have recently read.
- Visit your local library together. Tap into your child's interests. Reading isn't just about books: comics, sports reports, product instructions, street signs and posters – it's all reading.
- If a child or young person is struggling with literacy, getting her to write out the shopping list and recite it back to you in the shop or supermarket is a good way of getting her thinking about words without the pressure of being faced with a book or a piece of homework.
- There are lots of educational games that can be a way of helping your child to learn without them realising it.

Meeting the needs of unaccompanied young asylum seekers

Many lone asylum-seeking young people will experience problems accessing education related to the age they entered the UK, the time of year they arrived, the extent to which local schools are oversubscribed and how far foster carers and other professionals are active in the mediating process.

Help to improve English-language skills through access to English for Speakers of Other Languages (ESOL) classes is likely to be needed as well as additional support at home and at school/college.

The support you can provide as a foster carer is all important. For example, Muddah, a refugee from the war in Liberia, asked to change placement because his foster carers showed so little concern for his education and there was no place in the house where he could study. He was eventually moved to a family whose children were all at college or university and spent a lot of time talking to him about it. This reinforced his ambition to continue in education as far as he could go:

> *I'm not clever; I find studying very very difficult. I just work hard because I want to get somewhere, and my foster carer was very interested in my education. It was part of everyday life. Five days a week, Monday to Friday, every day she need to know my homework, she need to see my books, she need to speak to my teacher.*
>
> (Jackson and Ajayi, 2013, p.169)

Muddah went on to speak fluent English and flourish socially and academically with continuing support from his foster carers.

Generally speaking, carers and social workers seem to find that education is a high priority for these young people with few attendance problems once they are settled in an appropriate school or college.

Helping with homework

Sometimes it can be difficult to support children with their homework. Teaching methods have changed and we can't always help them as much as we would like to. It is important to discuss homework with your child. The amount will vary depending upon her age and you can assist her by supporting her to plan and organise the work she is given. Primary school children usually have daily reading and possibly spellings, and sometimes holiday projects to be completed. Secondary school children need a quiet space to work and will probably receive homework daily. Most schools have a system where you can check and see how much homework your child has, even if she is not bringing any home or says that she hasn't been given any. The homework may be listed in her planner so check this at least once a week.

Here is some useful advice from the agency Fostering Solutions:

> ***Set up a daily homework routine***
>
> *As with anything, the key to ensuring homework gets done is to have a set routine in place. This could be something as simple as each day, when they return from school, you sit down together and discuss what homework needs to be done.*
>
> *If the child isn't renowned for their honesty in this department then you can always contact the school to get an idea of how frequently homework is*

set. The teachers will be able to tell you which days your child should have homework and for which subjects.

Once you know what homework has to be done, you can either have them complete it before your evening meal, or straight after. Make sure you stick to whichever schedule you decide upon.

Do it together

Now, this doesn't mean take over and do the child's homework for them! Instead, sit down together and be there to guide them when necessary. Talk about the subjects they are covering. Actually discussing the homework and asking questions will enhance the learning process. They'll also likely be much more willing to do it if they aren't alone and it's turned into a more enjoyable task.

Ensure they have the right equipment

It is highly likely that your child is going to need access to a computer and the internet in order to complete their homework or undertake further learning around a subject. However, other learning tools can also come in useful such as an encyclopaedia, dictionary and thesaurus. While these can be found online, don't dismiss the usefulness of having physical copies too.

Providing further help

As well as helping them with their actual homework, it's a good idea to do additional things to enhance their learning, making their homework easier. Reading together, watching educational programmes, drawing and playing educational games can all help expand their learning capacity and enthusiasm for a subject.

Overall, helping your child with their homework doesn't just improve their education; it also helps the two of you to bond. Often foster children didn't receive a lot of support with things such as homework prior to being put into a placement, so just having you there to help will be very much appreciated – even more than you might realise.

(www.fosteringsolutions.com/news-events/back-school-helping-homework)

That said, if your child struggles with homework, even with your help, it may not be worth making a big issue out of it and possibly harming the relationship you are building with her. If homework is an issue in your house, talk to her class teacher about what support is available or could be put in place, such as a homework club. If it continues to be a problem, perhaps explain why you are not willing to force your child to complete homework if it is going to cause her a lot of stress.

Further tips to support learning

- Find a quiet place at home to use as a homework area.
- Ask your child how her teacher shows her how to work something out at school or what is the next step.
- Encourage your child to "have a go". Ask her if she can try a different way.
- Praise her for achievement, big or small!
- Give feedback rather than criticism. For example, say, 'That didn't seem to work' rather than 'You got that wrong.'
- Be patient and keep calm.
- Often schools have support such as a homework club or taster sessions for parents and carers on what children are learning and how they can be supported at home. Be sure to attend these.
- Discuss any homework tasks with your child and how it connects with what she is learning at school.
- Don't give your child the answer in order to get a task finished. Instead, explain how to look up information.
- Keep homework fun and make it a special time that you both look forward to.
- Talk about the things you found difficult when you were at school.
- Learn multiplication tables together.
- Don't allow it to become a big issue if the child really doesn't want to do it.
- Think of something positive for your child for when she has done it, such as playing a game together.

Supporting children and young people through exams

Secondary school pupils will need to choose a range of subjects to study in more detail for their GCSEs. Some subjects will be compulsory, such as English and maths, and others they will be able to choose. Schools differ in what they require as compulsory subjects. For example, some schools will require all pupils to take a language, others will not. You and your child will be given further guidance in Year 9 and you will be invited to attend an options evening to discuss the subjects with your child and their teachers. It is important that you attend these sessions to ensure that you support your child in making decisions that will help her career choices for the future.

Exams represent a snapshot of how your child has performed on the day and do not necessarily show what she is capable of within a subject. If she does not do as well as she had hoped, there are always other options to achieve her goals. Taking a different route or retaking exams is common. Reassure your child of this; options can be discussed with the head of year if needed.

Exam time can be stressful, particularly during GCSEs. Supporting your child can help to ease this.

Here are some tips:

- Provide a suitable quiet area for work away from family interruptions.
- Do not put too many demands on your child, such as doing household chores.
- Plan for revision with set times of no more than 45 minutes at a time.
- Ensure that regular breaks are included, with some relaxation time off.
- Make sure she is eating a good balanced diet including breakfast.
- Revise one subject at a time (with no more than two in one evening).
- Have all the materials at hand, such as books, notes, etc.
- Motivate her and be positive.
- Sleep is important, so early nights are recommended.
- Working with friends can help, it is good to talk through subjects and quiz each other.

- Making brief notes is much better than just reading through work.
- Research past papers as well as the examiners' comments on the exam boards' websites.
- Buy or borrow study guides for each subject if the school doesn't provide them.

Managing the internet, screen time and social networking

A survey by ChildWise revealed that school children spend an average of six hours a day in front of screens (TV, games consoles and online).

The internet has a huge influence on children and young people, both directly and indirectly affecting almost every aspect of their life. Much of this influence is positive, providing an essential tool for learning, building relationships and helping them find their place in the world. But what of the harmful side?

> *As a foster carer, dealing with a child's vulnerabilities in the online world is now as vital as it is in the real one.*

The National Fostering Agency (NFA), quoted above, has put together a comprehensive guide to internet safety for foster carers; it covers everything from the risks children face online, to the steps you can take to make sure the internet continues to have a positive influence on children in your care (see www.nfa.co.uk/blog/keeping-children-safe-online-foster-carer-guide-to-internet-safety).

For example, look out for signs of internet addiction, such as spending excessive amounts of time online, irritation when the internet is slow or switched off, poorer school performance, choosing not to go out socially in favour of online activity and spending money on games.

Some suggested strategies include:

- Try to reduce time online.
- Have set times when the internet is off in the home.
- Seek counselling or group support if the young person is willing to attend.

- Liaise with the school and ask them to insist on the young person attending revision sessions to limit screen time before exams.

In addition, below we include a slightly edited extract from *The Adopter's Handbook on Education* (Fursland, 2018) that applies equally to children and young people in foster care. The writer, Eileen Fursland, is something of an expert in this area, being the author of four BAAF guides to social media and online safety in relation to fostering and adoption (see References for details).

Social networking

The impact on children's lives of the internet and social networking is something that schools increasingly are having to deal with. As you will see in the next chapter, social networking as early as primary school has led to a rise in bullying as well as less obvious emotional risks to children and young people's well-being.

Some schools are taking the step of banning mobile phones in school because of the distraction and aggravation caused by young people using them for social networking in school. Even in primary school, issues of online safety are important – and even if the child in your care doesn't have a smart phone and you always supervise her at home when she is using the computer, her friends may well be showing her or introducing her to things that you would rather she did not see and remained unaware of.

Make sure you have parental controls on your internet provider to block pornography, gambling, websites that promote suicide, etc. You can also use these controls to limit internet use, for example, blocking gaming or chat at certain hours.

Parent Zone carried out a survey entitled 'The Perfect Generation: Is the internet undermining young people's mental health?' They interviewed young people and teachers and looked in-depth at the experiences of schools. This was the situation as seen by one school:

> *The internet and technology are identified here as factors exacerbating an already worrying situation. This school has seen pupils turn to the internet for affirmation, finding negativity or cruelty instead. They worry about pupils' inability to switch off from technology and desire to stay "in the loop", making them unable to take a break from social drama even when they are in*

> *their own bedrooms. They feel that their pupils are unable to find a balance between online and offline without reliable adult guidance.*
>
> *They have dealt with students looking up "dark" content about suicide and self-harm, but have also been troubled by worried young people turning to the internet for answers and coming back with unhelpful self-diagnoses. On the other hand, they have also started signposting some students in need of help to reputable websites, saying that much of the best available support is online. Again, they identify trusted adult guidance as the key in helping young people find helpful resources and avoid negative influences online.*

A second school in the survey also reported problems spilling over from social media into the school:

> *This school does not blame the internet for pupil mental health, but they do feel their pupils sometimes use social media as a platform to be unkind.*
>
> *For us, dealing with the aftermath when things go wrong, it's not the internet, it's social media. It's not the apps, it's what they do with them. They're mean to each other, they say mean things.*
>
> *While this has always been a part of teenage life, with the rise of mobile devices, it's become continuous – their students have lost the ability to disconnect for the night at home.*
>
> *They also see the internet as something that can validate negative behaviour, making bullying and nastiness seem acceptable because it's common and it's easy to do.*
>
> *These issues are also playing out with younger children, to the point where some pupils have "taken a step back" from technology by the time they are older. We heard that in this school, some teens even choose to come off social media because they don't want to deal with the negative side.*
>
> *The effect of the internet on their pupils varies based on maturity levels, friendship groups and, in their view most importantly, home lives.*
>
> (Rosen, 2016)

You cannot ban children and young people from the internet, though you may wish you could. The online world is a huge part of their lives. Many of them are only too well aware of the downsides of social networking, yet they are still prepared to put up with these in order to be able to enjoy the positives.

"Screen time" in itself is not necessarily bad for a child. Your child may be using the internet to research for homework, to collaborate on school projects, to find information on subjects she is interested in or to seek support from responsible websites. If a child is socially or geographically isolated, it can help her to connect and keep in touch with friends at a distance.

But too much time spent online might mean that children and young people are spending less time interacting with friends face to face or enjoying physical activities like games and sport, which are good for their mood and fitness. And children spending any amount of time online do need to learn how to stay safe, both to protect themselves from people who might pose risks of various kinds and to avoid getting into trouble through their own online activities. The more time they spend online, the higher the risk.

The child in your care may be more able than you to understand and use the technology but she is not necessarily emotionally mature enough to be able to cope with online risks and online interaction with other people.

There is a well-known disinhibiting effect of being behind a screen – people do and say things that they wouldn't do face to face. This can get people into trouble. Teenagers, in particular, are more likely to act impulsively and less likely to anticipate risks. Indeed, some may actively seek out risk for the thrill of it.

As a foster carer, like any parent, you need to recognise the risks: children can easily be exposed to online pornography, hate content, violent and disturbing images and videos, fake news, scams, sexting and live streaming, revenge porn, online grooming, gambling sites, cyberbullying, and pro-anorexia and pro-suicide websites.

Addiction to online games can be another trap, with some spending so long on their screens that it interferes with eating, sleeping, socialising and schoolwork. Online gaming or social networking into the early hours can leave young people feeling unable to "switch off", not getting enough sleep and consequently finding it hard to get to school and concentrate on lessons the next day.

Looked after children and young people who have difficulty forming friendships with their peers may be so keen to have friends that they are indiscriminately accepting of anyone who approaches them online. This can get them into trouble if they begin communicating with people who are out to exploit, bully or cause harm to others. Some end up being blackmailed and sexually exploited by people they have met online when they have gone along with their requests because they are keen to please and to make friends.

In some schools sexting is rife – young people see it as the norm. Girls are routinely asked to send explicit photographs of themselves. These can sometimes end up being circulated around the school and even more widely online. The child's school should help parents deal with this. If the image has been shared with other pupils, the school should have a process for dealing with it and will be able to help stop the image from being shared further. Social media sites should remove images like this if asked and the Internet Watch Foundation can work to get the picture removed from the internet.

The Internet Matters website has listed some of parents' most common concerns. It has advice about how to address these, along with advice on setting controls, filters and privacy settings and much more:

- *My child spends too long on their smartphone/tablet.*
- *My child has been sexting.*
- *My child has shared their personal information on social media.*
- *My child has a social media account but they are under 13.*
- *My child is using numerous social media platforms and I am not sure how to keep them safe.*
- *My child has been groomed online.*
- *My child is a cyberbully.*
- *My child is being cyberbullied.*
- *My child has seen porn online.*
- *My child is self-harming.*
- *My child has been radicalised online.*
- *Other people are posting pictures of my child online without permission.*

(www.internetmatters.org/hub/expert-opinion-child-online-safetyaddressing-top-parental-concerns)

Keep the lines of communication open (as far as is possible with a teenager, though this is rarely easy). Make sure you have two-way communication – if it feels like a lecture, your child will zone out. Try to ask and listen as much as you speak. Be genuinely interested in what she is doing. It won't be all bad!

Reassure her that you won't blame her or be cross if bad stuff happens to her online – that way, your child will be more likely to tell you or ask for help if she gets into difficulties.

It can seem overwhelming and some carers are tempted to give up and just let the child get on with it, but this is a really important part of fostering. Even if you are not technologically skilled, you can still show the child that you are concerned about what she is doing online and that you want to be "present" in her online life. That means talking with her about what she and her friends do online, taking an interest and discussing with her some of the difficult issues and things that can happen and asking how she would deal with them. It means setting rules and boundaries and ensuring that young people have information and awareness that will help keep them safe.

Educate yourself by reading the advice on the websites below, among others. Encourage your child to explore the e-safety sites – most of them have sections suitable for children of different ages, from very young children to teenagers, with games, quizzes, videos and other relatable information. Look at them together.

Here are a few to start off with:
www.childnet.com
www.internetmatters.org
www.thinkuknow.co.uk

Key points

- Talk with your child about school experiences and activities.
- Read together. Setting aside time to do this is about building closeness and trust as well as learning to decode words.
- Set up an area where your child can read and work undisturbed.
- Homework can be a struggle for any child and parent. If it becomes a big issue, talk to your child's teacher about what support might be available, such as a homework club.

- Unaccompanied young asylum seekers may be strongly motivated to succeed in their education but still need a lot of encouragement and support at home.
- Consider the quality and effect of children and young people's use of screen time and especially social networking. Talk to them about the use of privacy settings and how to stay safe online.

8 Moving between classes and schools

Transition

Beginning with separation from birth family, children in foster care typically have had to cope with one or more further moves. Transition is the moving from one stage of education to another: from one class to another or to a new school. It includes moving into an early years setting, from early years to a school reception, from Key Stage 1 to Key Stage 2, and from Year 6 (Key Stage 2) into secondary school. Each authority may have its own transition points, such as entering middle school at age eight.

Transition can be a time of fear, anxiety and unsettled feelings. The main requirement is to be prepared. Your child's school will make contact to advise on when the move will take place and pupils will be involved in meeting new teachers, settling into new classrooms and discussing new routines, such as changes in playtimes and expectations. For a looked after child, this can feel even more unsettling and more work may need to be done.

Extra transition meetings with school staff may be called for as well as additional visits to meet staff and explore the surroundings. Visual reminders of these experiences, for instance, using photos, can also help, as can opportunities for the child to express any concerns when he is at home with you. It is important to talk to your child about the changes ahead and raise any emerging issues with his teacher and school.

Typical changes may include:

- how your child travels to school;
- new timetables;
- different lunchtime routines;
- changes or removal of an afternoon playtime;
- more homework;

- new uniforms and equipment, such as PE kit;
- the need to develop greater independence for taking home messages.

Preparing your child

> *Major transitions, such as the start of a new school year or moving to a new school, as well as minor transitions such as moving from classroom to classroom or from school to home at the end of the day, can be challenging for many [foster] children. When a child has had times in her life when she has felt unsure or unsafe and lacked a sense of a "secure base", a transition can trigger the anxiety and fear she has felt before.*
>
> (Fursland, 2018, p.73)

The following strategies may help:

- Visit the new classroom or school.
- Spend additional time with a new teacher or inside a new classroom.
- Buddy up with a friend for transition.
- Meet new teachers in advance.
- Watch events at the new school, such as drama, sports or a class assembly.
- Attend open days and evenings where parents/carers meet new teachers.
- Make sure you have a school handbook to refer to.

Dealing with a child's separation anxiety

All children experience some degree of separation anxiety, often in relation to their first encounter with early education or school. This can be difficult to deal with, especially when it comes to looked after children for whom the process of change may well trigger memories of past trauma and separations and feelings of anxiety linked to loss.

The following suggestions may help:

- Practise separation. Leave your child for short periods of time.
- With young children, try and have separations after naps or feeding time. Small children are more susceptible to separation anxiety when they're tired or hungry.
- Develop a "goodbye" ritual. Rituals are reassuring and can be something as simple as a special wave or a goodbye kiss.
- Leave without a big fuss. Tell your child you are leaving and that you will return by a given time, then go; make the separation clear and swift.
- Minimise scary television. Your child is less likely to be fearful if the programmes you watch aren't frightening.
- Try not to give in. Reassure your child that he will be fine.
- Learn more about separation anxiety.
- Listen to your child and his feelings, let him talk about them and remind him that it was OK last time he was separated from you.
- Reassure your child that you will return.
- Anticipate when separation may be an issue and prepare for this.
- Have a consistent pattern for the day, talk to your child if this will change.
- Offer a choice where you can so that your child has some control; this might be through the choice of an activity when you arrive somewhere just after the separation.
- Stay calm even though you may find the situation stressful; make sure you have a chance to talk about it afterwards.
- If a child has been absent from school, help him to return as quickly as possible, even if this is for a shorter period of time.
- Praise your child whenever possible, even for small steps.
- Have a formalised plan. For example, to whom will you hand your child over? What activity will he do when he arrives?
- Consider a slightly earlier or later arrival when the first "business" of the day is not happening. Discuss with your school.

- Have a safe place where your child can go. Can he be dropped off in the reception area with an assistant, or is there a quieter place to go if he becomes anxious, such as the library or a separate room?
- At stressful times, a brief phone call home from your child may comfort him, a couple of minutes to reassure your child that you will see him later and he is doing a great job at school may help.
- Adult support from a school mentor and the time for your child to chat with him or her throughout the day may help.
- Other parents taking and fetching their children can also be a source of support.

The damage to a child's education, caused by separation anxiety, and ways of overcoming it are illustrated in the following case study about Ashley.

Ashley had begun a new school in Year 2. She had been in her new foster placement for just a few days and was finding it difficult to leave her carer (Mo), as she was worried that things might change again quickly. Ashley expressed this through not wanting to leave Mo or to stay at school.

The school drop-off was becoming increasingly stressful for Ashley, Mo and her teacher as she would cry, scream and run after Mo. The classroom was a busy place and mornings could be very hectic with lots of parents and carers dropping their children off and the teacher and teaching assistant busy settling everyone in. Mo was also worried about how it looked at school and what the other parents must think.

The teacher and carer arranged to meet and talk about strategies that could help Ashley. They came up with an action plan of things to try and discussed the reasons why Ashley was behaving like this. They decided to stick with the action plan for two weeks, keeping to the same routine and reassuring Ashley that Mo would return at the end of the day.

Actions:

- *Mo to bring Ashley to class 15 minutes early when the classroom was quiet and sit with her doing a joint activity.*
- *After 10 minutes, the teaching assistant would ask Ashley to help with a job, collecting resources from another area.*

- *Mo to say goodbye and reassure Ashley that she would return at the end of the day, after the last named lesson.*
- *Ashley had her own visual timetable and this was added to so that Ashley could see when Mo was returning.*
- *Mo to then leave – swiftly, firmly and consistently.*
- *If Mo was concerned whether Ashley had settled, she could call the school office once back home and check that all was well.*

Day 1 went very well for everyone; Ashley was delighted to be asked to help with a task and went off happily, a little hesitant, but much better than previously. Days 2,3, and 4 were a little more unsettled with Ashley more reluctant to go and help or to say goodbye. But Mo stuck with the routine and the firm and swift departure. As they moved into week 2, the routine became embedded and Ashley became more settled. This pattern stayed in place for half a term. The teacher and Mo then reviewed this and gradually Ashley was dropped off later at the normal school time, still with the distraction technique of jobs to be done in place.

The teacher thought:

'Bringing Ashley in a little earlier each day really helped with a calmer start to the morning and I think Mo was less anxious, too, as there were fewer people around if Ashley got upset.'

Mo commented:

'Sometimes I felt really upset for Ashley as I understood why she didn't want me to leave; she had so much change in her life recently. But her teacher was really good. I knew I had to be firm and consistent and keep to the same routine. Keeping her busy really helped until she settled in and made new friends, and became secure in knowing I would be returning to collect her.'

(Personal communication, 2018)

This example shows how important it is to sit and talk with teachers when something isn't going so well; they are there to support your child and you to settle into a new environment and routine.

Managing the move from primary to secondary school

Transition at any stage can be a very anxious time for a child, particularly the move to secondary school. This can be due to the potential change of friendship groups, vast changes to routines, and the need for rigorous organisation and independence. This will include children getting themselves to school, packing bags, doing homework in several subjects, transferring messages and letters home, joining after-school clubs and activities and getting to the right class at the right time. Throughout this, children will still need your support even if they don't ask for it. Children are preparing for later life, functioning in a busy world and sometimes they will not get this right; they will forget things and become disorganised. This is all normal. You may need to keep a lookout for your child and check in with him. For example, has he got everything he needs to be organised for the day?

Helping your child make the transition

Children will see many teachers at secondary school – probably more than 10 a week. They are unlikely to get on with all of them; encourage your child to discuss what is and isn't going well. If you are worried about a specific subject or lesson, make contact with the school, either with the teacher or the head of year to discuss your concerns.

The following suggestions are taken from *The Adopter's Handbook on Education* (Fursland, 2018, p. 106) but they apply equally to children in foster care.

- Ask your child how she feels about going to secondary school and talk through any of the issues that are worrying her. If she tends to be uncommunicative, try going for a walk or a long drive somewhere together– that can help some children to open up.
- Take her to visit the school at busy times and quiet times. Photos and/or a map of the school might help some children understand the new layout.
- Take any opportunity to go to the Christmas fair, summer fair or any other events the school or parent–teacher association puts on that are open to the public.

- If your child is anxious about travelling to school by public transport, have several practice runs. Agree that you will do the home–school journey together a couple of times, then again with you following a short distance behind, then when she is confident let her do it by herself (or with a friend who will also be going to that school).
- Cultivate your child's friendships with children who will be going to the same secondary school (and do the same with their parents!).
- Do role-plays with your child of any situations that you think she might find difficult, such as introducing herself to a new person or asking another child their name. Talk to your child about why she might want to keep her family history private, and role-play how she might respond if it comes up.
- Ask your child what she would like the teachers to know about her. If appropriate, involve her in putting together a profile that you can give to the school, or use what she has said when you are providing input into the Education Plan, if the school will be completing one of these for her.
- Be positive and enthusiastic about the new opportunities that the secondary school will offer – the range of sports, school facilities, the extracurricular clubs, bands, trips and other exciting things it has that primary school didn't.
- Help your child decide how she is going to say thank you and goodbye to her favourite people from her old school and help her to make cards and buy presents. Remind her that she can visit the school sometimes even after she has left.

Support and strategies for making new friends

Children may find it difficult to settle into a new school and make friends. With younger children, you can support this by discussing it with their teacher and other children in the class, and talking to other parents/carers, perhaps inviting their children around for a play date or meeting up at a play centre or park. Discuss with your child what makes a good friend and what he likes doing, facilitate joint games and activities. Children may also need help in explaining why they are in foster care when asked about this by other children

Older children can face further difficulties when they start a new school and join peer groups. Discuss with the school a buddying system for lunch and break times and see if some consistency can be found with other pupils who share their main lessons. Encourage activities after school through clubs connected within and outside the school.

Dealing with bullying

Bullying is not uncommon – incidents have escalated significantly since the advent of the internet and mobile devices – and you need to consider whether your child is affected or involved. If you have a concern, you must contact the school as there are procedures that will be put into place given that it is a safeguarding issue.

What is bullying?

There is no legal definition of bullying but most people think of it as a repeated behaviour that is intended to hurt someone, physically or emotionally. Some children and adults think that some name-calling may just be a bit of "banter" or that the child should "toughen up". If the child being targeted is unhappy with what is being said, then this should be followed up and treated as bullying. It is the perception of the victim that is important and he should be able to go to school without feeling unhappy or afraid.

Bullying can take different forms:

- taunting a child for being looked after;
- teasing;
- name-calling;
- making threats;
- physical assault;
- cyber bullying via text and social media such as instagram, twitter and snapchat.

It may also be of a particular nature, such as racist, homophobic, transphobic bullying or arising from the stigma of being in care. All schools must have a behaviour policy in place and within that (or separately) an anti-bullying policy.

Who can help?

If you suspect your child is either being bullied or is bullying another child, first make contact with your school. In the first instance this will be with the class teacher, tutor or head of year. If you find that the situation is not improving, then you must contact the head teacher and alert them to the issues.

Schools deal with bullying in different ways. They should have a way of recording incidents and may also have an intervention programme to discuss the issues with both the child being bullied and the child/children doing the bullying. Some local authorities may have a programme in place or a behaviour support worker who works with children around this issue and can support the school.

In some secondary schools discipline leaves a lot to be desired, sexual harassment is rife, and there are even incidences of sexual violence between children and young people. The Government has issued advice for schools and colleges on how to deal with this, covering:

- defining sexual violence and harassment;
- schools' and colleges' legal responsibilities;
- a whole school or college approach to safeguarding and child protection;
- how to respond to reports of sexual violence and sexual harassment.

(See www.gov.uk/government/publications/sexual-violence-andsexual-harassment-between-children-in-schools-and-college)

If you are worried for your child's safety, then you could call his social worker or the police (see www.gov.uk/bullying-at-school/the-law). Some names of charities that can support both you and your child in seeking advice and guidance are listed in the resources at the end of this handbook.

LGBTQ+ young people

If your foster child comes out to you as LGBTQ+[1] it may be advisable to talk to the school, especially if they may be trans. Schools have a duty to make sure young LGBTQ+ people are not being bullied so encourage your young person to tell a member of staff if this is happening or speak to the school yourself. The campaigning organisation, Stonewall, offers training to teachers on supporting LGBTQ+ students. Since 2007, Stonewall's 'Get Over It!' has helped tackle bullying in the classroom.

According to *The School Report* (Stonewall, 2017), self-harm and suicide are high-risk factors with more than four in five trans young people and three in five lesbian, gay and bisexual young people self-harming.

Help your young person to work out the best way to come out at school, college or university, if that is what they want to do. You may need to signpost staff to useful resources. Trans people are entitled to ask staff, colleagues and fellow students to use the name and gender pronoun of their choice.

If one of your other children is attending the same school as their LGBTQ+ sibling they may also experience difficulties from their peers. This may add pressure to the sibling relationship.

Legal implications

The Equality Act 2010 protects trans young people in schools, which means that they have the legal right to be referred to correctly and treated with respect in school. The Equality Act applies whether someone has undergone gender reassignment or whether they intend to, which means that young people who haven't medically transitioned are protected too.

All educational institutes will have an anti-bullying policy, which is there to ensure the well-being of every individual and should specifically include trans people and those who express gender variant behaviour. Find out more about dealing with bullying at: www.gov.uk/bullying-at-school/the-law. Details of recommended organisations such as the Anti-bullying Alliance are listed at the end of this handbook.

1 LGBTQ+ stands for lesbian, gay, bisexual, transgender and queer (or questioning) and others - see https://parentinfo.org/article/lgbtq-glossary-for-parents.

Key points

- Be prepared. Talk to your child about the changes ahead and encourage him to express his concerns. Be aware that the transition from primary to secondary school, with its new faces, potential change of friendship groups and wide range of teachers, can be particularly intimidating.
- Learn more about separation anxiety and the importance of consistency and rituals such as a wave or a kiss goodbye. Practise leaving him for short periods of time.
- Take him to visit the new school, to meet teachers and encourage friendships/contact with familiar children. Run through your experiences of going together, what you saw and the people you met.
- Don't hesitate to get in touch with the school in cases of bullying and/or sexual harassment. In cases of bullying related to a child or young person coming out as LGBTQ+ be aware that the Equality Act 2010 is in place to protect them.

9 Special needs, exclusion and alternative provision

Many looked after children have some kind of special educational need (SEN). This term applies to those who need additional support and extra help with making progress. They may have fallen behind with their studies for many reasons including physical, learning, behavioural, emotional or attendance problems. Some will have a wide range of difficulties and some will have a specific learning disability such as dyslexia or dyspraxia (further information can be found at www.gov.uk/children-with-special-educational-needs). Either way, they have a right to be educated within a mainstream school with other children.

Outcomes for looked after children with special needs

Statistics from 2017 state that:

- *Looked after children are almost four times more likely to have a special educational need (SEN) than all children and are almost 10 times more likely to have a statement of special educational need or education, health and care (EHC) plan than all children.*
- *In 2017, 56.3% of looked after children have a special educational need, compared to 45.9% of children in need and 14.4% of all children.*
- *Social, emotional and mental health is the most common primary type of special educational need for looked after children, covering 37.6% of those with a statement or EHC plan and 45.6% of those with SEN support.*
- *Looked after children with a statement or EHC plan are much less likely to have hearing impairment, visual impairment, autistic specturn disorder, physical disability, or speech, language and communication needs as their primary type of special educational need than all children.*

(Department for Education, 2017, p. 16)

What are special educational needs?

> *A child or young person has special educational needs (SEN) if they have a learning difficulty or disability which calls for special educational provision to be made for him or her.*
>
> (SEND Code of Practice, 2015, para xiii)

The Code of Practice goes on to define what is meant by a learning difficulty or disability. This is when a child or young person has a significantly greater problem in learning than the majority of others of the same age, or has a disability that prevents or hinders them from making use of mainstream school facilities compared with others of the same age.

This also applies to children over two and under school age, and to post-16 learning institutions.

Note that this is a broad definition covering a wide variety of learning needs.

These include:

- children and young people with moderate or profound learning difficulties, e.g. those with developmental delay, dyslexia, i.e. problems with reading, writing and spelling, and dyspraxia, i.e. difficulties with movement and co-ordination;
- children and young people with a physical disability that prevents them from accessing learning;
- children and young people who find it difficult to interact, form relationships and communicate, e.g. with insecure attachment or on the autistic spectrum, wide-ranging in itself;
- emotional and behavioural difficulties related to their upbringing that inhibit learning, interaction with peers, school attendance or settling in a classroom, for instance.

Such a wide definition might sound vague or indistinct. In fact, it enables a truly needs-based approach to be taken, treating every child or young person as an individual.

Principles

Underlying SEN provision is a number of principles that guide both the legislation and good practice. These will be familiar to you by now as they recur throughout this book. They set out the nature of the service children and young people should receive.

- Support is based on the particular needs of each individual child and young person.
- The views, wishes and feelings of the child or young person must also be taken into account. She should take part in decision-making. To do so, she must be provided with all necessary information and support.
- The views, wishes and feelings of parents and carers must be taken into account. They too should participate in decision-making and must be provided with all necessary information and support. (For a looked after child, the nature and extent of parental contributions varies according to her legal status.)
- Children and young people must be supported to help their development, to enable them to achieve the best possible educational outcomes and to prepare them for adulthood. To achieve this, you as a foster carer must be supported to ensure positive outcomes are achieved.

Good practice that follows from these principles supports:

- participation of children, young and carers in decision-making (as above);
- early identification of children and young people's needs;
- early intervention to support them;
- greater choice and control for young people and carers over support;
- collaboration between education, health and social care services to provide support;
- high quality SEN provision;
- a focus on inclusive practice and removing barriers to learning;
- preparation for adulthood, including independent living and employment.

Many schools and local authorities are doing excellent work but partly due to lack of resources, this foster carer's complaint is not unusual:

> *Our lad's been with us for over a year. He goes into school every day but he's not learning much. That's what I think anyway but the teachers say, 'Give him time, he's doing OK.' But you can tell – he doesn't retain information, something he goes through one day, next day it's like he's never seen it before let alone knows what to do. He's awkward with other children. No trouble in the class, by all accounts, but I don't think they notice him, the teacher leaves him alone but then he doesn't do anything. They don't seem to listen to me.*

You have a right to question, comment and complain if the above principles are not followed in practice. For instance, you must be actively involved in planning and decision-taking, you must be consulted, agencies should seek information about the child or young person from you, and you should be kept informed about the progress of the planning process.

Delays to the assessment of need and the provision of suitable interventions should be avoided. Inclusion is the right to be educated in mainstream school alongside children of the same age. Agencies should work together to meet the child's educational needs.

Assessment, planning and provision

Until recently, the term used to describe the child or young person's assessment was "a statement of special educational need", or simply "statement". The process was commonly called "statementing".

This has been replaced by the EHC plan or EHCP. Existing SEN statements will be converted into this plan. At the same time, children and young people with special education needs can receive support without it.

For looked after children, the PEP is key (see Chapter 3). Anyone who attends, including foster carers, should raise concerns about learning and unmet needs at the meeting. You are often in the best position to bring this up because you have a rounded picture of the child's needs, her behaviour and any other issues she is dealing with. You understand the child's anxieties, the things she enjoys, what troubles her and what she is good at. All of these and more may alert you to the possibilities that children need extra help to learn to their full potential.

The PEP considers all the relevant information and comes up with a plan to address needs. This includes asking for further information or assessments from other professionals to gain a complete understanding of the child or young person's needs. You can usefully prepare for this meeting by being ready to share the information they think is important. This may include detailed descriptions of behaviour as well as school-related information. Include anything you believe has an impact on the child or young person's well-being and therefore on her ability to learn.

The school's SENCO becomes heavily involved at this point. You should go out of your way to form a close working relationship with the SENCO, who will put together a plan to meet the child or young person's needs within the school (see Chapter 4). This plan can include resources from inside and outside school, and input from educational professionals ranging from learning support assistants to language therapists and educational psychologists. Ways of measuring progress and a timescale are also included.

Additional support may include:

- a special learning programme, such as maths;
- a nurture group to support social skills;
- using visual cards and timetables to help a child know what is happening during the day;
- specialist equipment;
- extra support from an assistant;
- small group work;
- someone observing and supporting in class or at play and lunchtime;
- assistance in taking part in classroom activities;
- help communicating with other children;
- support with physical difficulties such as eating, changing for PE or using the toilet.

These issues and ways of resolving them are illustrated in the following case study of Aaron's challenging behaviour.

Aaron had just started in Year 8 and he had been quite a challenging lad for the last couple of years. He would easily get distracted in class, be quite aggressive in his language and sometimes walk out of lessons. His school has put some strategies in place that Lisa and Joe, his carers, thought had been working quite well. But Aaron was now displaying more challenging behaviour at home and his carers were not sure how to tackle it. He was beginning to refuse to go to school on some mornings and then refusing to come off his play station in the evening. If this was enforced, he would become aggressive and Lisa and Joe were not confident to handle this.

Lisa and Joe discussed whether to contact their social worker or the school to see if anyone could help. They decided that contacting both would be best to see what help was available. When they called the school, they realised that Aaron's behaviour had become more disruptive there too, so it was not just a problem at home. The school suggested that they come in for a meeting so that they could explore together and with Aaron what might be causing the behaviour and how they could use similar strategies at home and school for consistency.

The teacher, Lisa and Joe all spoke to Aaron and found that one of the things contributing to his not wanting to go to school was that he was becoming fed up with some lessons and didn't like the subjects. He found some areas particularly difficult, such as English, and on days when he had this lesson would try to avoid attending. He was finding the subject increasingly difficult and had some clashes with the teacher over not completing homework. He stated he would much rather be at home on his play station! As his behaviour was becoming more challenging at home and school, his teachers thought it would be a good idea to seek further guidance and support from an agency that works with children with challenging behaviour. The school filled out the referral forms with Lisa and Joe's social worker and a behaviour support worker went into school to see Aaron in school and talked to his teachers. They also visited him at home with Lisa and Joe. The support worker then came up with a plan with strategies to provide support at school and home.

Joe commented:

'What was really key in things getting a little easier was communication; talking to the school really helped, knowing things were more difficult there too, and the fact that they were happy to get some professional support and advice made us feel better about seeking help.'

Lisa added:

'Yes, it was reassuring to know that we weren't on our own, we could ask for help and the school wanted to help us. The support worker was very friendly and helped us to be consistent with our strategies, even though at times it was difficult. She is still working with us and Aaron is having further help with his English.'

The support worker stated:

'Sometimes parents and carers don't want to ask for help, they feel as though they should know it all. But all children are different and things happen at different times, so it is good to ask for help when we need it, I still ask for help from colleagues now.'

(Personal communication, 2018)

How to deal with challenging behaviour in school

As we saw in Chapter 1, children and young people separated from their birth families, often for reasons of trauma, neglect and abuse, may well have trouble regulating their emotions and behaviours. Some find it difficult to function in school and at home and their underlying problems may be expressed by explosive outbursts due to grief and loss, frustration and anxiety. Their behaviour can take many forms and each needs to be considered individually as causes and remedies differ. Some manifestations are obvious, such as disobedience, tantrums and aggression, while others are less obvious but equally serious, such as withdrawal, phobia, anxiety, compulsive behaviour, enuresis or learning difficulties. Your child's school will have a behaviour policy in place which outlines the methods and strategies used when dealing with each of these problems and in some cases a specialist teacher, educational psychologist or other expert will be involved.

Serious breaches of discipline

All schools have to maintain order and normally start by using positive methods with praise and rewards given to children behaving in the expected way. These are effective for most pupils for most of the time. However, sometimes, children continue to display behaviour that is unacceptable and in such cases, schools will have further strategies in place. This may include "time out" in which a child spends some time in another classroom, or in secondary schools may include detention during a break time, lunchtime or at the end of the day.

It is important to note that these strategies can be damaging for children with attachment issues whom it is best not to isolate. Depriving them of a privilege isn't necessarily effective as they are used to deprivation from their previous experience and this compounds that lack of nurture.

If you would like further information on detentions, ask the school for a copy of their behaviour policy and speak to your child's form tutor or head of year if you would like to discuss the behaviour that is causing concern. Schools no longer need to give notice of an after school detention, but most schools do so to ensure that arrangements can be made for a child to get home safely afterwards. If behaviour issues escalate, then exclusion may be considered, and this is discussed further below.

Schools try to work with children to regulate their own behaviour, rather than to discipline them. However, on occasions additional strategies may be needed. For children who continually present challenging behaviour, a plan may have to be made that specifies the range of options for teachers to use along with the possibility of further professional support, such as referral to a behaviour support teacher who can support the child in school and/or at home.

Teachers are allowed to use reasonable force if needed to remove a child from a classroom, or to prevent a child from leaving. Most schools would avoid this is if possible, and some have trained teachers for using physical contact, if needed, in extreme circumstances. Schools are also able to search pupils' bags to check that dangerous or illegal items are not brought into the premises.

Exclusion

For a looked after child, exclusion should be seen as a last resort. If she is excluded, it is the virtual school's responsibility to find another school place or to secure a place in a Pupil Referral Unit (PRU) from day one of the exclusion, so she is not out of school.

PRUs are a type of school funded by the local authority to cater for pupils who need greater care and support than their school can provide. For instance, they may be:

- permanently excluded from their mainstream school for behaviour reasons, or at risk of permanent exclusion;
- experiencing emotional or behavioural difficulties, including problems with anger, mental health issues and school phobia/refusal;
- experiencing severe bullying;
- diagnosed with special educational needs or in the process of obtaining a diagnosis.

The benefits include access to highly trained specialist staff, small class sizes and timetables and subjects tailored to a child or a young person's specific needs. The downsides can be sharing a school with many other troubled children, a limited curriculum and not least, the stigma sometimes associated with PRUs. (A fuller explanation can be found at www.theschoolrun.com/what-is-a-pupil-referral-unit.)

Sometimes, pupils are internally excluded, so they are kept out of classes but will be set study tasks, usually in a classroom on their own or with other internally excluded children. Let the virtual school know of such incidents, so they can liaise with the school to try to prevent permanent exclusion. The young person may be eligible for support from a mentor, counsellor or educational psychologist. Take the example of Kim:

> *Kim, 15, was excluded from school for taking in a knife. She wasn't normally badly behaved and this action was out of character. She hadn't pulled the knife out on anyone but had shown it to some children in the playground and was spotted by a teacher. The school has a "no knives" policy, so it excluded her. She was moved to a Pupil Referral Unit for two weeks and then on to another school in the borough. She is now studying for GCSEs and hoping to go to a sixth form college to do a BTEC.*

The head teacher and teachers at a child's school may feel that the behaviour or problems that a child is presenting are unacceptable. They may, therefore, decide to exclude the child. This is normally for grossly challenging behaviour or a serious specific incident. Other provision, such as internal exclusion, increased mentoring, referral to an educational psychologist or CAMHS, social work visits, life story work, anger management training and safe spaces for a child to go to when she is feeling stressed should be considered. Reducing the number of GCSEs she is taking and/or private tuition at home may also help.

The school should notify you of any exclusion immediately, whereupon you should seek advice from the VSH. There are two kinds of exclusion: fixed-term and permanent.

Fixed-term exclusion

Fixed-term exclusion (FTE) (suspension) is for a set period of time, normally less than five days. It must not exceed 45 days in a single year and can only be authorised by the head teacher. For any exclusion over five days, she or he must make alternative arrangements and notify the parent/carer of what these are.

Any form of exclusion should be avoided if possible. Mossbourne Academy in East London credits the role of learning mentors for helping to keep down the number of FTEs:

> *One of the biggest factors at Mossbourne for ensuring that FTE rates for looked after children are low is the quality of the Learning Mentors at the Academy. The staff we have in those positions are highly skilled at developing a bond with the students who they see and form relationships built on trust. Through forming close attachments, our Mentors are able to note any changes in behaviours or concerns and can then inform relevant personnel so that key staff are equipped with information that will prevent situations from escalating. I have no hesitation in saying that our Learning Mentors are outstanding.*
>
> (Sarah Barron, Mossbourne Academy)

The responsibility for the child, while she is on a FTE, rests with the parent or carer. They are legally required to ensure that the child is not present in public places during school hours. This may mean that you will need to supervise her activity during the time of their exclusion (also see Chapter 10).

Permanent exclusion

Looked after children and young people are three times more likely to have an FTE and twice as likely as others to be permanently excluded from school.

Permanent exclusion occurs when a child will no longer be able to continue at the school she has been to. Your local authority will support you to find alternative school or education provision. This type of exclusion should only happen if other methods have been tried and are not working or a child has been involved in a serious first-time offence, such as violence or drug abuse.

Alternatives

There are alternatives to fixed-term and permanent exclusions. Some of these may have been used before or may be seen as a viable option. They could include removal of a child from class to a unit within school, a strategy that works with many children presenting challenging behaviour or with Social, Emotional and Mental Health (SEMH) difficulties. There may be an internal exclusion in which a child works in isolation away from her class, but is supervised by a member of staff. Lunchtime exclusions may occur if the challenging behaviour or incidents form a pattern at break times. Also, consideration of a temporary part-time timetable may be suitable if a child is struggling with integration.

Gifted and talented children

Inevitably, discussions of children's school difficulties tend to focus on the negatives, but what happens if your child's adjustment problems result from her being assessed as exceptionally able? Some children are classed as "gifted" "talented" or "higher learning potential", which means that they are either in or have the potential of being in the top group of children in their subject area. The term "gifted" tends to relate to academic subjects such as maths or history, whereas "talented" usually applies to subjects such as PE or drama. Higher Learning Potential (HLP) is a commonly used phrase that applies to any subject.

If your child is identified as having particular strengths in an area, then you may receive a letter from the school to let you know this. She may also have the opportunity to take part in additional activities, such as events with other school or trips with other children around a particular skill, such as leadership. The SENCO may oversee this group of children or the school may have a separate gifted and talented HPL co-ordinator. Children who are gifted and talented fit within the term "inclusion" as they are overseen to ensure that they are challenged and reach their potential and are protected from bullying because they stand out from others so clearly.

Key points

- All children with an SEN have a right to be educated within a mainstream school with other children.
- Special needs provision is guided by a specific set of principles and legislation including the proviso that parents and carers must be consulted at all times. The views of the child or young person must also be taken into account. Central to this process is the PEP.
- Only the head teacher can authorise an exclusion but the social worker, designated teacher and others are also likely to be involved. They must listen to you as the child's foster carer and see that you are kept informed of whatever is happening.
- Gifted and talented children need special attention too.

10 Post-16 education

Young people are legally required to stay in education or training until the age of 18. This can include one of the following: staying in full-time education; starting an apprenticeship or training; or spending 20 hours or more a week working or volunteering while in part-time education or training.

When choosing post-16 education it is a good idea to talk to teachers, careers advisers, social workers, other parents and students to learn from their experience. Unlike secondary schools, sixth forms can be selective and there are no preferential criteria for looked after children. Selection may be based on GCSE results, references and interview performance.

The virtual school may be able to provide advice on choosing a sixth form or apprenticeship scheme, based on their knowledge of the education provision and from talking to other foster carers and young people. If staffing levels allow, they may be able to accompany your young person on open days. You should at least have a meeting to discuss the options with your child's social worker.

Types of provision

Sixth forms

A sixth form attached to the child's current school would usually be the best option in terms of structure and pastoral care. This stability could be vital for a young person who has had multiple placement moves.

A sixth form attached to another school would also offer more pastoral care than a stand-alone sixth form college. Students are expected to work more independently at sixth form and will be given more free time. They usually don't have to wear the same uniform as the rest of the school but may be expected to wear smart clothes.

Charlene's case below illustrates some of the things that need to be considered when deciding what type of school or college to go for.

> *Charlene wanted to change schools and go to a mixed sixth form, as she was at a girls' school. Her foster carer Liz was worried about her leaving a school where staff had known her for five years. They went to open evenings and decided on another school with a sixth form rather than a sixth form college, so it would be more structured. Liz says: 'At least with it being a sixth form attached to a school, there was more structure and students were expected to be in school for six hours a day. However, it was harder to make friends as other kids who had been at the school for five years had their friendship groups. Charlene also had to establish new relationships with teachers.'*

Further Education colleges

Further Education (FE) colleges tend to provide a wider variety of subjects at A-level as well as the International Baccalaureate (alternative to A-levels offering a wider range of subjects, see p. 126), BTECs (professional qualifications related directly to the world of work) and the facility to re-sit GCSEs.

They generally expect students to be more independent and often only require that they attend their classes rather than staying in school for a set number of hours per day. Students can usually wear whatever they like.

This freedom may suit a more mature young person and the experience may be a better preparation for university. However, as looked after children are often less mature than their chronological age, this may be too much independence, too soon. Structure and boundaries can also help them to regulate their emotions so this could be an issue. Some, like Marco below, will probably do better staying on at school.

> *Marco, aged 16, wanted to leave his school and go to an FE college because he wanted more freedom. His social worker, Abi, advised against it, as her daughter attended the same college and was often sent home early and there was very little structure. Abi said: 'Marco needed more support to get him through his A-levels and would be better off staying in an environment where people knew him well. It was quite a battle to persuade him to stay at his school but I think it will work out better.'*

Others like Hayley may do well at FE college, especially with support:

A good example of the benefits of FE college is provided by care leaver Hayley, a 16-year-old special needs student who left school with two U [ungraded/fail] GCSE grades in Maths and English. She enrolled at entry level to study Routes to Animal Care. She spent 10 years in foster care but now lives at home with support from children's services because of her mother's special needs. A college course was seen as an important part of the plan to ease her return to her family but this was only made possible because her current mentor visited her school to meet her and manage the admission, which involved several meetings with Hayley's mother and social worker, the completion of the necessary forms, and the arrangement of transport. Naturally, the number of transitions involved in leaving school and returning home had made her very anxious and she was also nervous about starting college. So, she was paired with a fellow student on day one and there is continuous liaison with her social worker and support worker to keep her on track. She is now settled and keen to go on to a level 1 Equine qualification next year towards her chosen career.

(Herd and Legge, 2017, p. 71)

It is also worth noting that the staff employed by FE colleges tend to come from more diverse backgrounds than those working in schools.

Making the choice

Try to go to at least three open evenings at colleges and sixth forms. These should be held in the autumn term of Year 11. Check the deadlines for applying to each college. Check out the exam results on the institution's website and look at Ofsted reports. Find out about grades required to study certain subjects, talk to current students, ask about facilities for study and also for pursuing other interests such as music or sport. Find out about their pastoral care and provision for any special educational needs or disabilities. Attend a variety of talks at open evenings, exploring subjects the young person in your care may not have studied before, for example, sociology, business studies or law. Some sixth forms offer taster sessions to learn more about new subjects.

If the school or college is at some distance, make sure he can manage the journey.

Selecting your subjects

Think about the subjects your young person wishes to study and align these with his aspirations for future learning. For example, if he wants to study computing at university, does he need maths A-level? How many A-levels does he want to study? Most sixth forms encourage students to focus on three subjects, some allow four. Would a BTEC in a vocational subject suit him better? Or would he prefer a wider range of subjects as provided by an International Baccalaureate (IB)?

If he wants to go to a Russell Group university (representing the UK's 24 leading universities) he needs to choose at least two "facilitating" subjects at A-level. These are: English literature, history, modern languages, classical languages, maths and further maths, physics, biology, chemistry and geography.

If the young person wants to study more subjects, the IB Diploma programme is available at some sixth forms. All students must study six subjects, three at standard level and three at higher level over two years – including at least one foreign language. In addition, they study the theory of knowledge (TOK), complete an extended essay and undertake at least 150 hours of creative activity and service tasks outside of the classroom. (For more information see https://ibo.org/uk/students-parents/.)

If a vocational route would suit him better, BTEC (Business and Technology Education Council) might be a better option. BTECs are specialist work-related qualifications; they combine practical learning with subject and theory content.

A BTEC can be studied at level 2 or 3, either alongside academic qualifications or as part of a wider programme (such as an apprenticeship). There are over 2,000 BTEC qualifications across 16 sectors, including:

- applied science
- art and design
- business
- child care
- construction
- engineering
- media

- health and social care
- hospitality
- information and communications technology (ICT)
- horticulture/agriculture
- performing arts
- public services
- sport
- travel and tourism

(www.ucas.com/further-education/post-16-qualifications/qualifications-you-can-take/btec-diplomas)

How to apply

Most sixth-form provision requires an online application form. Students should fill this in themselves with your help. Make sure the young person emphasises any extra-curricular activities such as sport, work experience, music, awards, etc. The form usually asks about the young person's ambitions and why he wants to study their chosen subjects. Have a chat about the reasons and draft them on a Word document before filling in the form. The school he is attending will have to provide a reference and predicted grades.

Sula's story is yet another example of how valuable a foster carer's support can be.

Sula came into care aged 10 and was behind on all the national tests and very under-confident. After eight years in a stable and loving long-term foster home, she had the ability and courage to apply to university.

In Sula's words: 'I took every opportunity going and built up experiences that helped me to gain confidence.' Frances, her foster carer, says: 'My foster daughter had been on a trip to India with the virtual school, achieved her silver Duke of Edinburgh award through Police Cadets, gained some work experience and attended drama and cricket club. She came across very well on paper, and luckily, in person!'

Sula applied to five universities and was offered conditional places at all of them. She didn't get the grades for her first choice but secured a place at her "insurance" choice university.

Further support

Parents' evenings still take place at most sixth forms. PEPs are not statutory post-16 but are good practice. If they take place, they are supposed to be more student led in line with the young person becoming more independent.

It's a good idea to help with organisational and study skills as it can be a big leap from being spoon-fed at GCSE to being expected to learn more independently at sixth form and manage more "free" time. Help the young person to work out a timetable, especially in the run-up to exams.

Box files for each subject are a good way to help young people organise information and avoid losing handouts. A pin board for notices and timetables can also help them to remember meetings and help you to remind them.

The sixth form years pass very quickly; you will need to help your child to plan the next stage of his life, whether it is university, an apprenticeship or finding a job.

Apprenticeship schemes

Young people can apply for apprenticeship schemes as a way of gaining skills and experience while earning some money. A wide range of schemes across the private and public sector are available to all young people in foster care, with the exception of unaccompanied minors.

Training costs are funded by the government or employer. Apprenticeship schemes can run from one to six years and be at a range of entry levels from aged 16. They can also be combined with a degree (see www.gov.uk/government/publications/a-guide-to-apprenticeships).

The National Careers Service has advice on writing applications and what to do at interviews (nationalcareersservice.direct.gov.uk/home)

University doesn't suit everyone, as in Barbara's experience below:

Barbara, 18, a care leaver who had experienced anxiety and depression, still wanted to give something back and become a social worker. She went to university but struggled to cope without the structure of school and the support of a foster home. She had to give up but found an apprenticeship with a local council and is now in the final year of a two-year scheme. Her social worker says: 'University wasn't for her but she has flourished in a structured environment with the support of a line manager.' In her spare time, Barbara is also volunteering for a youth organisation.

18+ education: deciding the next stage

If your young person wants to stay in education beyond 18, you may need to help him choose the next stage of provision, which could include university, foundation years, apprenticeship schemes or studying abroad.

Start attending open days in the year before applying, from March to September. It's a good idea to plan some visits during the summer holidays. You may be able to get some financial assistance to attend.

Look at the institutions' websites as well as guides to universities and league tables (see resources listed at the end of this book).

The Sutton Trust (www.suttontrust.com/) runs free one-week summer schools at universities to encourage care leavers to go to university. These come highly recommended by Annie, aged 19 and now at Aston University:

I went to a Sutton Trust summer school at Nottingham University in the year before applying to university. I had taster sessions in Geography. I loved the experience.

Draw up a shortlist of institutions based on subject, ranking on league tables, distance from home, facilities, student reviews and any other criteria that are important to your young person. Think about courses that offer a year's work experience, sometimes known as a "sandwich" course.

How to apply

Students have to apply to university using a UCAS (Universities and Colleges Admissions Service) form. Make sure you know all the deadlines – for example, there are different ones for music, medicine, dentistry courses, Oxford and Cambridge, etc. Allow plenty of time to fill in the application form.

Get as much help as possible with the personal statement, showing it to teachers, friends, etc. It is a major selling tool. There are lots of tips about the application process online. It's important to tick the care leaver box as some universities offer guaranteed interviews for such young people (see www.thecompleteuniversityguide.co.uk/universities/applying-to-university-and-ucas-deadlines/your-ucas-application---tips-for-success/).

If your young person receives offers, he must narrow down his choice to a preferred and an insurance option, the latter generally asking for lower grades or even making an unconditional offer.

Before results day, make sure you have researched some alternatives in case he doesn't achieve the required grades and prepare him for mini-interviews over the phone. Go into the school or college to receive the results as early as possible. If the young person you are fostering needs to go through clearing, help him to research options, call universities, and mop up the tears – hopefully of joy when he secures a place. If he is offered a place at his "insurance" university but wants to try for a better one, he needs to reject the offer and go through clearing. Make sure he (or you) has called the preferred universities first to see if they would accept him and get it in writing by email before rejecting his "insurance" offer. This is a risky strategy but may pay off as it did for this foster carer:

> *My wife and I went into the school at 7.30 am with our foster son. He hadn't secured the grades he wanted, so we all researched like mad and started calling universities that were offering places through clearing. The phone lines are often engaged, so we were all trying to get through on three phones. Eventually, he secured a place and it worked out well in the end.*

Finance

Care leavers can apply for full student loans. Student Finance allows them to borrow an extra year of funding in case they need to repeat a year. They should also obtain a grant from the local authority and some universities have care leaver bursaries. These are often paid retrospectively, based on proof of attendance. Students often need to swipe their identity card as they enter lectures to prove attendance. Look out for other bursaries and scholarships and help your young person apply, keeping an eye on deadlines. For example, the Unite Foundation awards bursaries to care leavers offering free accommodation in their halls of residence for up to three years (www.unitefoundation.co.uk/what-we-do/).

Consider the financial implications for you and the young person of "staying put", living in catered accommodation or self-catering, either in halls or private accommodation. Some students may want to take a gap year. This can be a great opportunity but will have financial implications. If he is staying at home, he may be eligible for housing benefit – discuss all of this with your social work team.

"Staying put" arrangements

If you are offering "staying put", i.e. continuing your responsibilities as a foster carer after a young person turns 18, discuss whether he wants to carry on living at home or go away to university. If he goes away to university, staying put payments to carers are only made in the Christmas, Easter and summer holidays. Some councils pay students a grant towards accommodation but may expect the young person to contribute towards costs when he is staying at the foster home in the holidays. Discussions regarding staying put should have started from at least the age of 16 as part of the Pathway Plan.

Practical support

Before he leaves to go to university, make sure he has learned to cook at least four dishes and loaded a washing machine. Help him plan a budget for the term, taking him shopping so that he realises the cost of a weekly shop. Make sure he also understands all the options for safer sex. Once he leaves, your job isn't over – he may call frequently to ask questions and come home with dirty laundry! As looked after young people often have attachment issues, they may struggle to form or keep friendships, find the lack of structure a challenge and like most students, go a bit wild in the first year. They may also think they are fully independent and grown-up, so reject your advice. Try to be there for him in whatever capacity he needs: a shoulder to cry on, a walking encyclopaedia and an extended loan facility. . .

Tanita's case is just one example of the positive impact that a caring adult can have by continuing to support a young person through further or higher education.

Tanita, 17, an asylum seeker without full leave to remain, became depressed. Sonia, a learning manager from Hackney's virtual school team, worked with her, building up a relationship, helping her to fill in forms and going with her to interviews. Sonia managed to get Tanita on to an access to nursing course and to help her gain some work experience as a care worker. Once her leave to remain came through, Sonia supported her to secure a place at university. Sonia has kept in touch with her during her studies and Tanita told her 'because of you, I'm able to have a positive impact on other people'.

Education in custody

Young people are supposed to receive 25 hours of education time in custody, but this is usually private study rather than tuition. Even this is often reduced if staff numbers are low and supervision can't be guaranteed so prisoners are restricted to their cells. Exams can be taken in custody and the virtual school should be able to supply workbooks and other educational material. There can be some training opportunities; for example, in Feltham Young Offenders' Institute, young people can get training in food hygiene, construction and customer service.

Sometimes young people can be released on temporary licence or under the escort of a prison guard to take exams. The virtual school should be involved in liaising with the prison to make sure the young person is receiving educational support. This can include holding a PEP in the prison. In London, Hackney's virtual school has a book club so young people can order books to read while in prison.

The virtual school should also hold a pre-release meeting and make sure that a resettlement plan is in place within five days of release, so that the young person returns to some form of education, employment or training. The school may also help with interview skills, speech and language support and signposting to useful organisations.

These two case studies again show the importance of continuing support, this time for two young men with experience of prison.

Lee

Lee, 16, was remanded in custody in the run-up to taking his GCSEs. The virtual school sent him education packs and teachers visited him in prison to make sure he had work to complete. His exam papers were sent to a secure training centre so that he could sit the exams. He passed three GCSEs and was offered a resettlement meeting within five days of release. He is now training to be a plumber.

Salman

Salman, 17, came out of prison on bail and was allocated to Sonia, a learning manager from Hackney's virtual school team. He had been arrested for driving without insurance or a licence.

Sonia says: 'I used to meet with him regularly and could tell when he had been smoking cannabis. He had difficulties with trust issues and keeping appointments. He said he was interested in getting into construction as a career. I found him an opportunity to work for a surveying company. He needed a lot of support at first but he stuck at it. I went to court with him and the judge agreed to give him a suspended sentence to allow him the chance to turn his life around. He progressed to become a supervisor on a construction site and hasn't re-offended in two years.'

(www.gov.uk/government/publications/custody-and-resettlement/custody-and-resettlement-section-7-case-management-guidance)

Key points

- Young people are legally required to stay in some form of education or training up to the age of 18. Entry to the school's sixth form is usually dependent on GCSE results; the other main options are FE colleges and apprenticeship schemes. Talk to teachers, careers advisers, social workers, other carers/parents and students to learn from their experience.
- As a foster carer, your support continues to be important – from helping young people to choose which route to take (academic or vocational) to navigating the online application process and preparing them for the practical aspects of leaving home. Basic life skills such as budgeting, cooking, doing laundry, etc. don't always come naturally!
- Virtual schools should also provide continuing support with education, even if a person is in custody.

Conclusion: things to remember

Given the previous histories and instabilities experienced by many looked after children, it is hardly surprising that so many of them fail to fulfil their educational potential. This is a tragedy because, as explained in the introduction, education is an important factor in enhancing children's prospects and the role of the foster carer is vital in this. Providing the support that children need to develop into successful and happy adults is a huge and demanding task. Education is a vital element of this. Carers need to understand the role that it plays in child development, to not to be afraid to seek help and advice when required, and to stand up and advocate for the child or young person when things get difficult. If you feel you need help, then do ask. Schools are very willing to help. Building positive relationships with the school will help to secure a successful and fulfilling future for your child.

Remember:

- Education will help your child have a positive work and home life in the future.
- Work with schools to support your child: they want her to achieve the best she can. Listen to school staff and talk to them when you have concerns.
- Keep in regular contact with your child's teacher.
- If your child is in primary school, read with her daily.
- Attend parent/carer evenings with your child so that she and the teachers can see that you are interested in her work and you are all working together.
- Attend other events, such as class assemblies, summer fairs and sports days, which are an important part of sharing school life.
- Know what is happening in school; check for letters and respond to them.
- Check all homework is being completed and help your child when needed.
- Listen out for any signs of bullying, either direct/face-to-face or via social media.

- Ensure that your child arrives at school on time each day.
- Expect your child to become anxious or stressed during testing and exam times; give reassurance and decide how best to give support.
- Encourage her to stay on in education and/or training for as long as possible.
- Make sure she is aware of all the options available and support her to apply for a place once she has decided on the initial path she would like to take.
- Try to have high but realistic expectations for her to help her believe in herself.
- Encourage your friends and family to talk to her about their experiences of education and employment, for example, how did they become a teacher, plumber, etc.
- Help her to build up her outside interests, which will be good for her as a whole and look good on her personal statement or CV.
- Encourage her to be as organised as possible and help her to file and keep important papers; note down important deadlines and application dates.
- Build in enough time to visit schools, colleges and universities in the year before she has to apply, so that it is not a big rush.
- If she is very resistant to doing homework or letting you support her, liaise with the school, as they may be able to persuade or insist on a child attending homework club or revision sessions.
- Celebrate all your young person's success by framing certificates, taking photographs of her holding them, which you display prominently in your home, so visitors can admire her success and boost her self-esteem.

Great expectations

Having listed some of the main points that we hope you will take from this handbook, we end with a positive story from a young woman who defied early negative experiences and expectations to achieve educational success.

By the age of 13, Collette Isabel Bentley had experienced nine changes of school and as many placement moves. It was only by chance that she eventually found "new parents" who supported her education and encouraged the ability and aspirations that led to a place at university and finally qualification as a medical doctor. In this edited extract from her chapter 'Great expectations: supporting "unrealistic" aspirations for children in care' (Jackson, 2013, pp. 45–52), she describes the difference that having foster carers who supported her education made to her life.

> *Two weeks after moving in, my new foster carers took me shopping for a school uniform, a French dictionary and a hole punch, and drove me the 40-minute car journey across the city to school, with the expectation that whatever was going on in my home life, I would not only go to school but also achieve my potential.*
>
> *There was not only an expectation that I would attend school, be courteous to teachers, learn my spellings and establish functional friendships; it was assumed that I would do this irrespective of what obstacles continued to my way. For someone like me, who was desperate to shake off the shackles of an identity that had been forced upon me ("the poor kid in care who has no hope"), it was liberating. Indeed, I would go so far as to say that it was the key to my salvation. I believe the most rewarding approach to caring for a child like me, scarred from an early age by emotional, physical and intellectual abuse, is one that offers a supportive hand, a leg-up, but ultimately expects the same as would be expected from any other child.*
>
> *It would be misguided to suggest that a good education constitutes a panacea for all the woes of a looked after child, but I do maintain that what we expect of children educationally is often a marker of our broader expectations of them and for their future, and consequently colours our entire approach to how we raise them.*
>
> *Although my new foster carers were highly educated, which helped in my particular case, this is not a prerequisite for providing a foster child with the support necessary to achieve recovery and fulfilment through education. Time and time again, my education was a vehicle through which my "parents" transmitted a crucial message: 'You are worthy of our time, love, care and expectations.' As a child who had been rejected and abused, humiliated and shamed, it was overwhelmingly invigorating to have an adult care enough to learn my French vocabulary, with me, to buy me the right PE kit so I wouldn't have to face humiliation at school and to stand in the rain on a Saturday morning to cheer for me to win the 100-metres sprint at the inter-school competition.*

This kind of support had an immediately positive effect on my general attitude towards life. My social worker at the time approached me several years later and recalled how my behaviour had seemingly changed overnight. In reality, of course, it took a lot longer. But gradually the gregarious, determined extrovert that I had once been came back and I eventually started to expect things of myself. Slowly my hopes and dreams were rekindled and eventually I went on to achieve a first-class honours degree at university, get married and train as a doctor.

References

Bergin C and Bergin D (2009) 'Attachment in the classroom', *Educational Psychology Review* 21, pp. 141–170.

Bomber L (2007) *Inside I'm Hurting: Practical strategies for supporting children with attachment difficulties in schools*, Duffield: Worth Publishing.

Bond H (2016) *Thinking about Fostering ? The definitive guide to fostering in the UK*, London : CoramBAAF.

Brown J (2015) 'The challenges of caring for a child with FASD', *Adoption & Fostering* 39(3), pp. 247–255.

Children's Commissioner (2017) *Assessment of the outcomes of vulnerable children*. Available at: www.childrenscommissioner.gov.uk/wp-content/uploads/2017/07/CCO-TP4-Assessing-Vulnerability-Outcomes-Cordis-Bright-1.pdf.

Department for Education (2014) *Children looked after in England (including adoption and care leavers) year ending 31 March 2015*. Available at: https://assets.publishing.service.gov.uk/government/uploads/system/uploads/attachment_data/file/464756/SFR34_2015_Text.pdf.

Department for Education (December 2014b) *School Admissions Code: Statutory guidance for admission authorities, governing bodies, local authorities, schools adjudicators and admission appeals panels.* Available at: www.gov.uk/government/uploads/system/uploads/attachment_data/file/389388/School_Admissions_Code_2014_-_1.

Department for Education (December 2014a) *Advice on the admission of summer born children for local authorities, school admission authorities and parents*. Available at: www.gov.uk/government/uploads/system/uploads/attachment_data/file/389448/Summer_born_admissions_advice_Dec_2014.pdf.

Department for Education (2017) *Outcomes for children looked after by local authorities in England, 31 March 2017*. Available at: https://assets.publishing.service.gov.uk/government/uploads/system/uploads/attachment_data/file/695360/SFR20_2018_Text__1_.pdf.

Department for Education (February 2018) *The designated teacher for looked-after and previously looked-after children: Statutory guidance on their roles and responsibilities.* Available at: www.gov.uk/government/publications/designated-teacher-for-looked-after-children.

Department for Education (March 2018) *School exclusions review: terms of reference.* Available at: www.gov.uk/government/publications/school-exclusions-review-terms-of-reference.

Donovan S (2016) 'How social worker and teacher combined to turn around my son's education', *Community Care,* 18 May.

Donovan T (2017) 'Two-thirds of schools without mental health champion', *Children & Young People Now*, 21 December. Available at: www.cypnow.co.uk/cyp/news/2004664/two-thirds-of-schools-without-mental-health-champion.

Fursland E (2011) *Foster Care and Social Networking*. London: BAAF.

Fursland E (2013) *Facing Up to Facebook : A survival guide for adoptive families*, London: CoramBAAF.

Fursland E (2018) *The Adopter's Handbook on Education: Getting the best for your child*, London: CoramBAAF.

Herd R and Legge T (2017) 'The education of looked after children: the social implications of further education', *Adoption & Fostering* 41(1), pp. 67–74.

Jackson S and Ajayi S (2013) 'Foster care and higher education'. In Jackson S (ed.) *Pathways through Education for Young People in Care*, London: BAAF, pp. 159–173.

John B (2017) 'The big decision', *SEN Magazine,* Sept–Oct, Issue 90.

Local Government and Social Care Ombudsman (2017 'A disproportionate burden': families struggling with new special educational needs system when councils get it wrong. Available at: www.lgo.org.uk/information-centre/news/2017/oct/a-disproportionate-burden-families-struggling-with-new-special-educational-needs-system-when-councils-get-it-wrong.

Marshall N (2018) 'Focusing on attachment', *SEN Magazine*, 8 January. Available at: https://senmagazine.co.uk/home/uncategorised/focussing-on-attachment.

Mather M (2018) *Dealing with Foetal Alcohol Disorder: A guide for social workers*, London: CoramBAAF.

Nock J (undated) 'In a class of their own', *SEN magazine*. Available at: https://senmagazine.co.uk/home/articles/senarticles-2/in-a-class-of-their-own.

NOFAS-UK (2017) *Teaching a Student with FASD.* Available at: www.nofas-uk.org/TeachingAStudentWithFASD_FINper cent20REV.pdf.

OECD (Organisation for Economic Co-operation and Development) (2014) *Education Indicators in Focus*. Available at: www.oecd.org/edu/skills-beyond-school/.

Pallett C, Simmonds J and Warman A (2010) *Supporting Children's Learning: A training programme for foster carers*, London: BAAF.

Rees Centre (2017) *Principles for the Alex Timpson Programme on Attachment and Trauma in Schools,* Research Programme. Information available at: http://reescentre.education.ox.ac.uk/research/alex-timpson-attachment-and-trauma-programme-in-schools/.

Rivers S (2018) 'Supporting the education of looked after children: the role of the virtual school head', *Adoption & Fostering* 42(2), pp. 151–161.

Rix K, Lea L and Edwards A (2017) *Reading in Foster Families: Report*. London: Book Trust/National Children's Bureau. Available at: www.booktrust.org.uk/globalassets/resources/research/reading-in-foster-families-full-report.pdf.

Roberts B (2015) '"I know that I'm in my own world; it's OK, they know me here": the challenge of coping with FASD in educational settings', *Adoption & Fostering* 39(3), pp. 235–246.

Roberts K (2009) *Early Home Learning Matters: A good practice guide*. London: Family and Parenting Institute.

Rosen R (2016) *'The Perfect Generation': Is the internet undermining young people's mental health?,* Parent Zone. Available at: https://parentzone.org.uk/sites/default/files/Theper cent20Perfectper cent20Generationper cent20report.pdf.

Stonewall (2017) *The School Report: The experiences of lesbian, gay, bi and trans pupils in Britain's schools.* Available at: www.stonewall.org.uk/resources/school-report-2017.

Treisman K (2017) *Working with Relational and Developmental Trauma in Children and Adolescents*, Oxford: Routledge.

Walter S (2016) Early experiences in the neurosequential model in education, *The Canadian Journal for Teacher Research.* Available at: www.teacherresearch.ca/blog/article/2016/10/30/314-early-experiences-in-the-neurosequential-model-in-education.

Useful resources

Where foster carers and schools can get information, advice, training and support with education issues

The Fostering Network

https://afaeducation.org/free-dt-resources/

The Fostering Network has resources, training, publications, and advice lines to help foster carers make the most of educational services and opportunities available to them.

Fosterline

www.fosterline.info/

Tel: 0800 040 7675

Provides confidential, impartial, advice information and signposting on the broad range of issues of concern to foster carers and those interested in fostering, in order to support them in their role, aid retention and encourage recruitment. Funded by the Department of Education.

Coram Voice

coramvoice.org.uk

Advocacy service for children in care, incorporating advice, support and problem-solving to ensure that children's voices are at the heart of service delivery. They also run an advocacy helpline (Tel: 0808 800 5792).

The National Youth Advocacy Service (NYAS)

nyas.net

Rights-based charity that operates across England and Wales for children, young people and adults. Services include a national advocacy helpline (Tel: 0808 808 1001), a peer mentoring scheme and the provision of independent visitors for children in care.

Attachment aware schools

www.attachmentawareschools.com

This is a partnership between Bath Spa University, the National College for Teaching and Leadership, the virtual schools of Bath and North East Somerset and Stoke on Trent and the training organisation Kate Cairns Associates (led by attachment specialist Kate Cairns) and schools. It trains teachers, heads and school governors to be "attachment aware".

On its website, there are resources from the Attachment Aware Schools training programme and a list of trainers and organisations that are able to work with schools to develop greater attachment awareness. All the materials are informed by research and based on evidence from classroom practice.

Trauma-informed Education

www.traumainformededucation.org.uk

An education pathway incorporating Touchbase, DDP (Dyadic Developmental Practice) and Theraplay. These three organisations propose that once whole school communities have had training in the area of children's attachment needs, two strategic pastoral members of staff are chosen. They will then lead on and facilitate both advocacy, and support interventions on behalf of children and young people who have suffered relational trauma and loss.

Trauma-Informed Schools UK

www.traumainformedschools.co.uk

Aim to provide appropriate training for schools, communities and organisations so that they become trauma informed and mentally healthy places for all.

Emotion coaching

www.emotioncoaching.co.uk

Emotion coaching is an approach used to support children and young people with their behaviour and mental and emotional well-being. It emphasises the importance of considering the emotions underlying behaviours "in the moment" before dealing with setting limits and solving problems.

The aim is to de-escalate difficult situations, increase children's and young people's understanding of their emotions and support their emotional regulation. This involves five steps in this order: tuning in, connecting, listening, reflecting and problem-solving.

Some schools have introduced emotion coaching as a peer mentoring programme, with selected older pupils being trained to use it with younger pupils.

FAGUS

www.fagus.org.uk

FAGUS (Fostering Attachment awareness to Generate Understanding in Schools) is a framework for measuring the attainment of goals for children in areas that fall outside the academic curriculum.

It is a resource for assessing, monitoring and supporting children's emotional and social development and measuring their progress in these areas. It outlines the developmental processes in a child's social and emotional development across 13 different domains, which include: awareness and understanding of others; self-control; motivation and self-efficacy; and moral development. This allows you to identify at what age level a child is functioning and his or her strengths and weaknesses across each domain.

Teachers can then focus specific interventions to encourage social and emotional progress and measure the child's success.

NOFAS-UK (National Organisation for Foetal Alcohol Syndrome) UK

www.nofas-uk.org/

Information, training and resources for people affected by FASD, their parents, carers and professionals. The organisation has some useful resources for teachers and teaching assistants. It will also try to help parents/carers who call with queries about children's education.

Inner world work

www.innerworldwork.co.uk

This is an online resource centre for parents and carers, offering a collection of free, high quality resources to support parents, carers and children who are trauma-experienced. These include information sheets on *What Survival Looks Like in Primary School, What Survival Looks Like in Secondary School,* and the *Whole Class Happy Pack* of practical, easy, free, grounding and relaxation ideas for teachers to use on a daily basis to create a safer, happier classroom environment.

IPSEA

www.ipsea.org.uk

Independent Parental Special Education Advice (known as IPSEA) offers free and independent legally-based information, advice and support to help get the right education for children and young people with all kinds of special educational needs (SEN) and disabilities. IPSEA gives advice and support on:

- local authorities' legal duties to assess and provide for children with special educational needs;
- exclusions of children with special needs/disabilities;
- action/inaction by local authorities and/or schools that discriminate against children and young people with disabilities.

Nurture groups

www.nurturegroups.org

Nurture groups are an intervention used with vulnerable and disadvantaged children and young people and those who have social, emotional and behavioural difficulties, for instance, those who are withdrawn or aggressive, have low self-esteem, are disengaged from learning or who won't stay in the classroom.

They are in-school classes of six to 12 children or young people in early years settings or primary or secondary schools. Two teachers run the group, providing warmth, acceptance and nurturing experiences to help remove the barriers to the children's learning and help them develop positive relationships with teachers and peers. There is a lot of emphasis on communication and social learning. As well as regular lessons, activities include emotional literacy sessions, sharing news and eating breakfast together.

Children attend nurture groups often on a part-time basis but remain part of their main class group and usually return full-time to their own class within two to four terms.

The most common way to fund nurture group provision in the UK is through the Pupil Premium.

Mentally Healthy Schools

www.mentallyhealthyschools.org.uk

Information, advice and resources to help primary schools understand and promote all children's mental health and well-being.

Advice on bullying

Anti-bullying alliance

www.anti-bullyingalliance.org.uk/

Bullying UK

www.bullying.co.uk/general-advice/

Childline

www.childline.org.uk/Explore/Bullying/Pages/Bullyinginfo.aspx

Kidscape

www.kidscape.org.uk/

LGBTQ+ young people

Beaumont Society

www.beaumontsociety.org.uk/

Provides help and support for the transgender community.

Gender identity development service (GIDS)

TavistockandPortman.NHS.UK/

Run by the Tavistock Clinic, GIDS is for children and young people, and their families, who experience difficulties in the development of their gender identity. It's a national specialised service, based in London and Leeds.

Gendered Intelligence

http://genderedintelligence.co.uk/

Gendered Intelligence supports young trans people aged eight to 25. It has produced a guide with trans young people and their parents. It includes useful information, stories and quotes.

Mermaids

www.mermaidsuk.org.uk/

Mermaids operates a helpline aimed at supporting transgender youth up to and including the age of 19, their families and professionals working with them.

Stonewall

www.stonewall.org.uk

Campaigning group for the LGBTQ+ community.

New Family Social

www.newfamilysocial.org.uk/resources/getting-help-support/transgender/

Offers support for LGBT adopters and foster carers.

Education resources and websites

UCAS

www.ucas.com

The Universities and Colleges Admissions Service administers applications to Higher Education. It includes information on choosing courses and links to university websites.

UK Course Finder

www.ukcoursefinder.com

Helps you find a university course.

icould

www.icould.com

Features careers advice and a test to match your personality to potential careers.

Apprenticeships UK

www.apprenticeships.org.uk

Government site giving information about choosing an apprenticeship.

Do-it

www.do-it.org

Volunteering opportunities to boost your child's work experience.

The Complete University Guide

www.completeuniversityguide.co.uk

League tables and profiles of universities.

The student room

www.thestudentroom.co.uk

A space for GCSE, A-level and university students to share academic and social knowledge. This includes examples of UCAS personal statements.

Unistats

www.unistats.direct.gov.uk

Official statistics on UK universities including highest rated university by subject and average entry grades.

Student finance

www.gov.uk/student-finance

How to apply for student finance.

Whatuni?

www.whatuni.com

University and degree course comparison website.

Uni Compare

https://universitycompare.com/advice/student/choosing-sixth-form-college/

Choosing a sixth form college.

Success at school.org

https://successatschool.org/advicedetails/470/Five-Practical-Alternatives-to-Going-to-University

Alternatives to university.

Types of school

www.gov.uk/types-of-school

School admissions

www.gov.uk/schools-admissions/admissions-criteria

Curriculum

www.cie.org.uk/programmes-and-qualifications/cambridge-primary/cambridge-primary/curriculum/

www.greatlearning.com/ipc/

Special needs and inclusion

www.gov.uk/children-with-special-educational-needs

www.gov.uk/children-with-special-educational-needs/special-educational-needs-support

www.gov.uk/children-with-special-educational-needs/extra-SEN-help

www.gov.uk/special-educational-needs-disability-tribunal/overview

Attendance

www.gov.uk/education-attendance-council

Prospects

www.prospects.ac.uk

Useful information about choosing a career, including a questionnaire. Information about gap years, studying abroad, interview tips.

Care leavers

Become

www.becomecharity.org.uk/

A charity supporting care leavers.

Coram Voice

coramvoice.org.uk

Advocacy helpline: 0808 800 5792

Focuses on care leavers' rights and making sure they get the help they need.

Propel

https://propel.org.uk/UK/

Website for care leavers who want to go to university.

Rees Foundation

www.reesfoundation.org/what-we-do

A charity supporting care leavers.

The Care Leavers' Foundation

www.thecareleaversfoundation.org/

Provides small grants for care leavers.

Further reading

Attachment in the Classroom: The links between children's early experience, emotional wellbeing and performance in school
Heather Geddes, 2006, Worth Publishing.

Educating Children and Young People with Fetal Alcohol Spectrum Disorders
Carolyn Blackburn, 2012, Routledge.

How to Transform Your School into an LGBT+ friendly place
Elly Barnes and Anna Carlile, 2018, Jessica Kingsley Publishers.

Inclusive Strategies to Support Pupils with Attachment Difficulties Make it Through the School Day
Louise Michelle Bomber, 2011, Worth Publishing.

Inside I'm Hurting: Practical strategies for supporting children with attachment difficulties in schools
Louise Michelle Bomber, 2007, Worth Publishing.

Overcoming Barriers to Learning: How a culture of care in schools helps troubled pupils to learn
Sheila Mulvenney, 2017, Worth Publishing.

Ten Top Tips on Supporting Education
Eileen Fursland with Kate Cairns and Chris Stanway, 2013, BAAF

Therapeutic Parenting in a Nutshell: Positives and pitfalls
Sarah Naish, 2016, CreateSpace Independent Publishing Platform.

Appendix: Different types of schools

Infant, junior and primary schools

- Infant schools educate children from the ages of 4 to 7.
- Junior schools follow on from infant schools and provide for children aged 7 to 11.
- Primary schools cover both age ranges under the same school, from aged 4 to 11 years.
- The first year of school is called the reception year, and is for children aged 4 to 5 years.
- Children then move into Year 1, followed by Year 2. This is known as Key Stage 1 (KS1).
- Children then move into Years 3, 4, 5 and 6. This is known as Key Stage 2 (KS2).
- Some children may start school the term before they are five years old.
- Some schools have one entry point and all children start in the September of the school year in which they reach their fifth birthday.
- The legal age that a child must attend school is five years.

Middle schools

- In some parts of England, such as Suffolk and Dorset, there is a different school system that runs across the age ranges and this includes middle schools.
- The first school educates pupils aged 4 to 8 years, the middle school runs for 9- to 13-year-olds, and the upper school teaches 14- to 16-year-olds.

- In some areas, middle schools are being phased out and replaced with the primary and secondary school system.

Secondary schools

- Secondary schools are for pupils aged 11 to 16 years old.
- Some young people will stay at their secondary school to do A-levels at sixth form until they are 18 or 19 years old.
- Some will go to another school, may attend an FE college or may start an apprenticeship or another form of training when aged 16 years (see below).
- Grammar schools are secondary schools run by the council, a foundation body or a trust. They select all or most of their pupils based on academic ability and usually require an entrance exam to be taken the year before. For information on grammar school entry, you will need to see your local authority guidance.

Free schools

Free schools can be primary or secondary and cater for all abilities. They are funded by the Government but not run by the local authority. As a result, they can set their own pay and conditions for staff, change the length of school terms and the school day, and do not have to follow the National Curriculum.

Faith schools

- Faith schools are like other primary and secondary schools but may well give priority to an applicant who is of the same faith as that of the school.
- If they are not bound by the National Curriculum, they are free to teach only about their own religion.

Academies

- Academies are publicly funded independent schools.
- Academy chains are a group of schools forming part of an overall Academy trust.
- Academies can be primary or secondary schools and Academy trusts may include a mixture of both.
- Academies do not have to follow the National Curriculum but often do.
- Academies can set their own term times, so these may differ from other local schools.
- Academies still have to follow the same rules on admissions, Special Educational Needs and Disabilities (SEND) and exclusions.
- The current Government has pledged that all schools will convert to academies by 2020 and head teachers and teaching unions are currently discussing this.

Special schools and additional provision units

- Special schools include schools that have provision for children with additional needs or disabilities.
- Entrance into these schools will be through a child's Education and Health Care (EHC) plan.
- Pupils have more individualised support for their needs.
- Pupil Referral Units (PRUs) support children who do not attend mainstream school due to exclusion, behavioural needs or pregnancy.
- Many pupils at a PRU are school refusers or excluded pupils who find mainstream schools difficult.
- PRUs may offer part-time and full-time education.
- PRUs may be used as part of a short-term or longer-term plan.

Private and independent schools

- There are both primary and secondary private or independent schools.
- They may be run as girls- or boys-only schools, or be co-educational (both boys and girls mixed).
- Parents or guardians pay for schooling that is likely to cost several thousand pounds a term.
- Private and independent schools may be day attendance or boarding schools, or a mixture of both.
- Schools are registered with the Department for Education and are inspected.
- Like free schools and academy schools they do not have to teach the National Curriculum.
- They may also follow a particular faith.
- They may have scholarships or bursaries for disadvantaged pupils.

Further education

- Further education (FE) runs from 16 years to 19 years old (see Chapter 10).
- FE may be at a school sixth form where most pupils study for A levels.
- FE may be at a college where pupils may study for an alternative qualification, such as a diploma, BTEC up to level 5 or NVQ.
- FE may include apprenticeships, which include a training allowance combined with a qualification (see www.gov.uk/apply-apprenticeship).

Higher education

- Higher education (HE) runs from 18 years and above.
- HE includes qualifications such as an undergraduate degree or diploma, and post-graduate courses.

- Entry requirements vary, and consideration to this should be given when planning FE courses and qualifications.

Glossary

Acronyms and special terms used in education can be difficult to get to grips with. Here are some commonly used terms.

A level	Advanced level (exams taken at 18 years of age)
CLA	Children looked after
CRB	Criminal Records Bureau (previous check made to ensure that staff are OK to work with children)
DBS	Disclosure and Barring Service (current check made to ensure that staff are OK to work with children)
DfE	Department for Education (Government department)
EHC plan	Education and Health Care plan
EWO	Education welfare officer
FSW	Family support worker, may also be family liaison worker
GCSE	General Certificate of Secondary Education (taken at 16 years of age)
G&T	Gifted and talented
GNVQ	General National Vocational Qualification
HLP	Higher learning potential
HOD	Head of department (in a secondary school or further or higher education)
ICT	Information and communication technology
IEP	Individual Education Plan
KS	Key stage
LAC	Looked after children
LA	Local authority

LSA	Learning support assistant
MFL	Modern foreign languages
MLD	Mild learning difficulties
NC	National Curriculum
NVQ	National Vocational Qualifications
NQT	Newly qualified teacher
Ofsted	Office for standards in education (inspectors of schools)
PSP	Pastoral Support Programme
PEP	Personal Education Plan
PMLD	Profound and multiple learning difficulties
PRU	Pupil Referral Unit
SATs	Standard Assessment Tests
SEBD	Social, Behavioural and Emotional Difficulties
SEN	Special Educational Needs
SENCO	Special Educational Needs Co-ordinator
SLD	Severe learning difficulties
SpLD	Specific learning difficulties
UCAS	University and College Admissions Service